D0295701

FALKIRK COMMUNITY
TRUST LIBRARIES

The Mysterious World of Cats

CANCELLED

The Mysterious World of Cats

What magic, myth, shamanism and science teach us about their secret powers

HERBIE BRENNAN

CORONET

First published in Great Britain in 2017 by Coronet
An imprint of Hodder & Stoughton
An Hachette UK company

1

Copyright © Herbie Brennan 2017

The right of Herbie Brennan to be identified as the Author
of the Work has been asserted by him in accordance with
the Copyright, Designs and Patents Act 1988.

All rights reserved. No part of this publication may be reproduced, stored
in a retrieval system, or transmitted, in any form or by any means without
the prior written permission of the publisher, nor be otherwise circulated
in any form of binding or cover other than that in which it is published and
without a similar condition being imposed on the subsequent purchaser.

A CIP catalogue record for this title is available from the British Library

Hardback ISBN: 978 1 473 63805 1
Ebook ISBN: 978 1 473 63806 8

Typeset in Cochin by Hewer Text UK Ltd, Edinburgh
Printed and bound by Clays Ltd, St Ives plc

Hodder & Stoughton policy is to use papers that are natural, renewable
and recyclable products and made from wood grown in sustainable
forests. The logging and manufacturing processes are expected to
conform to the environmental regulations of the country of origin.

Hodder & Stoughton Ltd
Carmelite House
50 Victoria Embankment
London EC4Y 0DZ

www.hodder.co.uk

To Broccoli Cat One, The Maggot, Wug-Wug, Wobber, Charismatic Banana and all the other cats, past and present, who have enriched my life

Falkirk Community Trust	
30124 03077874 2	
Askews & Holts	
398.2452	£10.99
MK	

Contents

Preface: Schrödinger's Cat

It was a Viennese physicist, Erwin Rudolf Josef Alexander Schrödinger, who first discovered the most astounding of all the mysterious talents exhibited by cats.

In 1935, Professor Schrödinger was living in Oxford with two women – one his wife, the other his mistress – and a cat called Milton. That he got away with the unconventional domestic arrangement would suggest he was far cleverer than the average man, but his intelligence was clearly underestimated by Milton, who should have realised his master was following a line of enquiry that must eventually reveal to the world catdom's greatest secret.

This was what happened, without going into the mathematics of the situation . . .

There are three kinds of physics nowadays: Newtonian physics, which helps you understand how your world works; relativity theory, which helps you understand how the universe works; and quantum mechanics, which explains the nature of small things and helps you understand absolutely nothing at all.

Why do we love cats so much?

The quantum model has spread its net wider and wider and had so many of its findings experimentally confirmed that scientists now routinely refer to it as the most successful physics theory ever.

But there are problems.

Take atoms. When I was a boy, scientists imagined an atom as a miniature solar system: electrons orbited a nucleus the way planets orbit the sun. Except that electrons don't orbit like planets. They jump from one orbit to another *without crossing the space in between.*

Take sub-atomic particles. There was a time when these were thought of as very tiny cannonballs. And so they are. But they're also waveforms, *both at the same time.*

Take quantum foam. The smallest, most fundamental building blocks of our entire physical universe *appear out of nowhere* for a moment, then disappear again.

Take the chair you're sitting on. *It's not actually solid*. You are only able to sit on it because of the interaction of electrical fields.

Take the world you're living in. There's a genuine possibility it will vanish – with you in it – before you reach the end of this page. It's not very likely, but it's possible.

Take the structure of reality. *It changes if you look at it*.

You'll have noticed something about all these examples. They don't make any sense. They didn't make any sense to Schrödinger in 1935 either, but that didn't inhibit him from working on them – particularly the last one about reality changing if you look at it. He was engaged in a lengthy correspondence with Einstein at the time and neither of them was happy that their fellow physicists were interpreting the evidence properly.[*] Eventually Schrödinger came up with the idea of creating a 'thought experiment' to show how ridiculous the current theories really were.

He asked us to imagine a cat shut in a box with a 50 per cent likelihood of triggering a lethal poison. When you opened the box you would, of course, find the cat either dead or alive. *But*, demanded Schrödinger,

---

[*] Einstein said he simply couldn't believe the universe would change just because a mouse looked at it.

rhetorically, is it sensible to imagine that, until the reveal, the cat is hovering in a dimension somewhere between life and death?

To his astonishment, the overwhelming majority of his fellow physicists answered yes. Because the consensus conclusion, known as the Copenhagen interpretation of quantum physics and supported by many of the finest minds of our time, is that cats have a secret zombie power permitting them to be alive and dead *at the same time.*

And it's not the only secret they've been harbouring. For generations, cats have been associated with the occult and supernatural. They are surrounded by dark superstitions. A black cat crossing your path is a herald of good luck. But beware of crossing a black cat's path for then the luck will be all bad. The cat of any colour is widely regarded as the boon companion of the witch, riding proudly on the back of her broomstick as she flies to her wicked sabbat meetings with the Devil. The cat sometimes walks with the gods – she draws Freya's chariot in Norse mythology – but she is more often remembered as the pet of Hecate in Hell. Why such a fearsome reputation wrapped up in such a sweet and cuddly animal? And might it in any sense be justified?

These are the areas this book sets out to explore by focusing on one central, critical question: why are cats the most popular pet on the planet? Or, put another

---

* Physicists don't actually use the word 'zombie' but that's what they mean.

way, why do humans love cats the way they do? Both versions of the question are deceptively simple, but by using them as a jumping-off point, we will quickly find ourselves deeply embroiled in the mysterious world of cats, facing a perplexing array of puzzles. In our attempts to find our way out of the maze, we shall seek clues in legend, myth, folklore, conventional history and even science. We shall examine some strange byways and shall not hesitate to speculate where speculation is needed.

The book begins with a thorough examination of what we know for sure about the average domestic cat. But it quickly becomes obvious that this little animal is far from average. And so we are sucked gently into the mystery.

Why do we love cats as we do? The answer is as unexpected as it is profound.

Introduction

I once owned a cat called Pablo, a pure white neutered tom with pale blue eyes and a gormless expression.

Somebody told me that white cats with blue eyes carried a gene that made them prone to deafness. I don't know if this is generally true, but it certainly applied to Pablo. If you approached him from behind and touched him, however gently, he started violently. If you crept up on him and banged a pair of cymbals – as I once did, experimentally – there was not so much as a twitch of an ear. Pablo was obviously as deaf as a post.

Pablo and I lived together in a rented wing of an Irish country house, located in a 350-acre pastoral estate. One evening around twilight, I was seated by a window admiring the view when Pablo appeared on the scene. He walked purposefully to a wall that edged a part of the courtyard and sat down. Then he peered upwards into the darkening sky.

I craned to see what he was looking at, but there was not so much as a raindrop in his line of vision. Then Pablo did that amazing thing only cats can do. From a seated position, he jumped six feet straight up in the air. When he came down again he had something winged and fluttering in his mouth. I thought it was a bird, but when I went out to investigate, I found it was a bat.

Only the pure in heart can hear the bat's squeak. The folk saying has a solid foundation. When you are a child (and presumably pure in heart) your hearing is wide-ranging and acute. But as the relentless years roll on, you lose the ability to listen in the higher registers. So you can no longer catch every word the pretty girl is saying at the drinks party, and you become totally deaf to the whole sonic world of the bat.

But deaf old Pablo, with his recessive gene, white fur and pale blue eyes, could hear bats perfectly, as he later proved by catching scores of them. Their echolocation chirps and squeaks were as visible to him as if he had a sonar screen built in between his ears. Yet, as far as he was concerned, my clashing cymbals remained mute.

I'd venture to suggest all cats are like that. Just when you think you know them, they produce an ability or behaviour as enigmatic as the far side of the moon. There is a mystery about cats that reaches back to ancient times. I have shared my life with them for more than seven decades. I know whereof I speak.

By the time you finish this book, so will you.

The Fundamental Question

In my youth, I kept seventeen cats in a single-bedroomed flat. You opened a cupboard and cats would fall out. There were cats in my bed, cats on my chairs. The food bill was crippling, but I loved every one.

Seventeen cats seems a lot to me, now my menagerie is down to three, but it transpires not to be the most that anyone has harboured. A woman in Cornwall has posted a notice on her front door alerting visitors to the fact she expects them to leave the most comfortable chairs free for her army of thirty-four cats. There is a woman in Siberia – Nina Kostova – whose small apartment is home to a happy 130.[*] From Israel comes news that in 2012 a man petitioned to divorce his wife on the grounds that she refused to give up any of her 550 cats. He told the court he was unable to sleep because cats constantly occupied his bed. They also blocked his access to bathroom and kitchen, and when he sat down

---

[*] https://www.youtube.com/watch?v=o3hhCh9t-bI

to eat, they jumped onto the table and stole his food.* These examples are the tip of an iceberg. Cats today are the most popular pets on earth, outnumbering their nearest rivals, dogs, by a margin of millions.

The statistics raise a question: what evolutionary or social pressures linked the fates of Felidae with *Homo sapiens* so firmly? The answer, when you begin to think of it, is not particularly obvious. When Wolf evolved into Dog he paid for his food with love, loyalty, biddability, enthusiasm, entertainment and assistance in herding the sheep. Humanity, for its part, fed, sheltered and protected him. In short, there were benefits for both sides. But where is the human benefit derived from living with *Felis catus*, who pays for his food by demanding more, then turns it down because what you've provided – at considerable expense† – isn't to his liking now, although he adored it yesterday?

And where is the human benefit derived from the large numbers of feral cats who sun themselves in the ruins of the Roman Forum and Colosseum? Far from treating them as pests, the Italians have taken them to their hearts, and volunteers risk scratches and bites to feed them and provide medical attention. The treatment of feral cats in Rome and elsewhere underlines the

---

* UPI report: http://www.upi.com/Odd_News/2012/05/27/Couple-split -over-wifes-550-cats/UPI-98981338138685/?st_rec=92141342368115 Accessed April 2016.
† Where I live, it's cheaper to feed cats on roast chicken than pouches of cat food. Unfortunately some of mine don't *like* roast chicken.

mystery of our reaction to them. A common approach is to neuter, immunise and mark – usually by nicking the tip of one ear – an individual feral, which is then returned to its wild ways with one important advantage: the cat is assigned a human volunteer to feed and care for it for the rest of its life.

Genetic examination indicates that domestic cats are the descendants of *Felis silvestris lybica,* the African wild-cat, but ten thousand years of evolution have done little to change their basic nature. Unlike the wolf, whose partnership with humans produced benign variations in temperament, and physical mutations into dogs ranging from the Saint Bernard to the Chihuahua, the cat has remained essentially unchanged in both temperament and looks. It is, if we are prepared to face the facts, a ruthless killer implicated in the extinction of thirty-three bird species,[*] and the living embodiment of arrogance and cupboard love in its relationship with humanity. The personality of the average cat is neatly encapsulated in the cartoon that depicts a conversation between a cat and a dog in which the cat is saying, 'I was a dog in my past life, but I decided to come back as a god.' The essential difference between dog and cat is underlined by another telling joke about our pets' reactions to us. Dog says, 'You feed me, you shelter and protect me. You must be a god.' Cat says, 'You feed me, you shelter and protect me. I must be a god.' As Churchill

* http://en.wikipedia.org/wiki/Cat Accessed November 2015.

aptly put it, dogs look up to us, cats look down on us. We should not, could not, love such a creature, and yet we do. The fundamental question is *why*?

When I first set to writing a book that might answer this question, I thought the job would be easy. After all, I'd had cats – always more than one – as my constant, intimate companions from early childhood. In the event, it proved the most difficult book I've ever written. Part of the problem was the cats themselves, who refused to be herded on the printed page as stubbornly as they do in real life. Another part was the utterly unpredictable behaviour of human beings when it comes to cats. Who would have guessed we might appoint one a railway-station master . . .? But the real difficulty, I eventually discovered, was that I failed to take the question seriously enough. I thought in terms of slick, witty answers, whereas the reality was something far more profound.

And more than a little weird.

A Portrait of Your Cat

'Is that a ferret?' asked a visiting workman when confronted with the cross-eyed gaze of my seal-point Siamese.

'Don't be stupid!' admonished his companion. 'That's a Pekinese cat.'

Visiting workmen aren't the only ones with a limited knowledge of *Felis catus*, the classification first appended to domestic cats by the biologist Linnaeus in 1758. Cats are enigmatic to the point of the uncanny. They attract more superstitions than common sense – the lucky black cat . . . (in Japan, the lucky cat of any colour: they even have cafés packed with cats for you to stroke while you drink your morning coffee) . . . the witch's cat . . . the terrifying wampus cat of North American folklore . . . But before we delve into these mysterious realms, let's begin with a few certainties about the average house cat, although I would be prepared to bet a small sum of money there are at least three important things you don't know about the purring bundle of fur that greets you with her tail up every morning. (Unless, of course, she has something better to do.) Here, then, for your education and edification is a portrait of your puss.

She weighs between nine and ten pounds, unless she's a Maine Coon, which weighs as much as twenty-four pounds, or a freak that can weigh as little as two. While there's obviously a size difference between males and females, the average house cat stands between nine and ten inches tall and has a body length of eighteen inches, plus a further twelve for the tail. (Except for Manx cats, which have no tails worth mentioning.)

Whether or not you're comfortable with the thought, your cat is a killing machine, with lots of evolutionary developments designed to make her an efficient predator. She can pass through any space where she can fit her head, due to the free-floating collarbones attaching forelegs to shoulders, which, incidentally, allow her to turn those forelegs in almost any direction. She walks silently on her toes, attempting to place each hind paw in the print of the corresponding forepaw to minimise sound and visible tracks. You probably haven't noticed, but when she does walk, she moves both legs on one side of her body before moving the two legs on the other side, like a camel or a giraffe. You can entertain yourself by making a riddle of this little-noted fact: *Why is a cat like a camel? Because she walks like a giraffe.* But be sure you say 'walks' because, confusingly, when your cat breaks into a run, it's the diagonally opposite hind and forelegs that move simultaneously.

When she catches her prey – usually a small bird or rodent – she plays with it, allowing it to break free of her clutches before catching it again and again. This pattern of behaviour is rooted neither in sport nor in sadism, but is a means of exhausting the prey so it succumbs to the eventual kill easily and without danger to the cat. The kill itself is typically carried out with a single lethal bite to the back of the neck that severs the spinal cord, causing paralysis and almost instant death. Big cats – lions, tigers, leopards – usually kill in much the same way, although they don't play with their food beforehand.

The exertion of hunting will never cause your cat to break into a sweat, or not in the way we would understand the term. Her only sweat glands are in the pads of her paws. Fortunately, she doesn't need a whole lot more for two main reasons. My alpha feline, a plump, pretty queen named Broccoli Cat One (after a cardboard box), squeezes underneath our blazing wood stove in the winter, thus illustrating that cats remain comfortable at skin temperatures that would send us running for an ice pack. Specifically, you and I start to worry when our skin temperature hits 38°C/100°F. Your cat, by contrast, will scarcely twitch a whisker before she reaches 52°C/126°F. When it does get too hot, even for her, she cools down mainly by panting.

Although your cat is well qualified to survive by eating her prey, this will not stop her demanding that you provide her with additional nourishment at inconvenient intervals. You may feel appreciated by the way she guzzles it, but much of her reaction is due to the fact she doesn't chew. God has provided her with thirty teeth – sixteen at the top, fourteen on the bottom – but all of them are quite useless for chewing, and many of those lining the cheek don't even meet when her mouth is closed. When she finds meat, she uses her canines and molars to shred it, then swallows it.

The type of food you decide to feed her is important, not just because cats are fussy eaters but because some types of proprietary cat foods are actually damaging to your cat's health. Your cat has a short intestine and her stomach juices are not much good for digesting anything other than meat. You can't feed her an all-meat diet, which is unbalanced and can lead to deficiency diseases, but you do need to think in terms of a meat-based, low-carbohydrate approach, although you'll probably need to visit a dedicated pet store to get it.

You're in for a few surprises when you begin to investigate what really is a healthy diet for your cat. For example, you'll never again be able to use that old expression about the *cat who got the cream*. Despite the age-old tradition of offering kitty a saucer of milk, it turns out cats are lactose-intolerant – the sugars in milk can give them diarrhoea. Not that they care much for any sugars in the first place: their taste buds are so few – about five hundred compared to your nine thousand – that they are unable to taste sweetness. Talking of which, you should also be aware that chocolate is as toxic to cats as it is to dogs, although cats are less likely to eat it.

This may be a good time to mention that cats are even more at risk from the toxins of modern living than we are. Some things on the avoidance list are obvious, such as rat bait, but you might not so readily think of keeping your cat well clear of

- House plants such as philodendrons and the Easter lily, which can cause fatal kidney damage.
- Mothballs.
- Ethylene glycol, a common antifreeze. Cats love it and a spoonful can kill them.
- Onions and garlic, toxic in large quantities.
- Essential oils, particularly tea tree and commercial products, like shampoos, containing it.
- Phenol-based household cleaners and disinfectants.
- Human medicines, particularly painkillers containing paracetamol, which can be fatal even in very small doses.
- Shellfish. Many cats are as allergic as humans, with just as unfortunate results.

Adult cats can't suck. They're unable to close their lips properly, which is why they lap liquids instead of slurping them like we do. In case you ever want to try it, you lap by touching the tip of your tongue to the surface of the liquid, then pulling it back quickly. This has the effect of drawing up a small amount of liquid, but by lapping at a rate of four times a second, your cat can get a decent drink in a reasonable time.

After eating and, less often, drinking, your cat will typically give herself a thorough wash. To aid with the task, nature has provided her with a set of what are called papillae, stiff, hooked, backward-facing spines growing on her tongue. These act as a hairbrush for her fur and anything else she decides to wash, including you, if she thinks you are lovable, dirty or tasty enough. Your cat is so supple she can tuck her leg behind her ear and lick her own bottom, occasioning my paternal grandmother to remark severely, 'You'd never catch me doing that!'

A man and his cat, by Edward Lear

Some sources I consulted insist the reason cats groom so frequently is a bit of a mystery. Cat-lovers tend to believe their pets have discovered cleanliness is next to godliness. My own inclination is to accept what I was told as a child: cats groom to remove any scent that might warn prey of their approach. But, whatever the reason, grooming often leads to an accumulation of fur balls in your cat's stomach. When this becomes troublesome, she will eat grass, which acts as an emetic and helps her sick up the offending accumulation on the seat of your favourite armchair.

Once she is well fed, watered and groomed, your cat may signal her state of mind by purring,* particularly if she can find a patch of sunlight to recline in. Purring develops in kittens as a signal to the mother that they want to be fed and carries through to adulthood largely as a signal of contentment. You can feel the mechanism that drives the sound by placing one finger lightly on her throat, but science took a while to figure out exactly what it is. At one time, they thought it arose when the cat somehow made the blood rumble around in its chest, but that theory has been largely abandoned now. The breath seems to be involved in making the sound, because, if you listen very, very carefully, you can hear a difference between the in breath and the out breath, with the barest hint of a pause between the two. But what actually

---

* In rare cases, purring can signal pain, although there are usually other signs of distress present.

happens is that the vocal cords are being vibrated by a special set of muscles. Ever a complicated animal, your cat will often hum at the same time, something that does indeed involve the breath. If you happen to own a particularly cunning cat, she may modify the purr by adding a sort of miaowing sound to give it a sense of urgency. This usually means she *really* wants feeding.

They used to think purring was confined to domestic cats, but this is nonsense. I once listened to a tiger purr, a sound as magnificent as the animal himself. Lions, according to my research, can purr too.

As the purr fades, or even if it doesn't, your cat will make herself comfortable and, in all likelihood, fall asleep. Cats spend most of their lives asleep – anything up to twenty hours out of twenty-four, with an average of somewhere between thirteen and fourteen. When they sleep, they dream. Some experts insist that they don't, because they sleep too lightly. But while light sleep is true enough – the slightest stimulus will wake a cat – my money remains on dreaming. You can see the rapid eye movements (REM sleep) behind closed lids and feel sporadic muscle twitches – both indicators of dreaming – while your cat is asleep on your lap.

When your cat is awake, you will probably find her in or near your home, except during the hours of darkness when she may venture abroad to do a little hunting. Cats, particularly unneutered toms, are fiercely territorial – another characteristic they share with big cats in the wild – and can establish property rights to ranges up to sixty-nine acres (about twenty-eight hectares.) When your cat rubs her head fondly across your ankle, she's not so much showing affection as marking you as her property. The same gesture, which awakens scent glands in the side of her head, is used to mark the boundaries of her territory, and you should count yourself lucky she did not choose either of her two other markers, spraying urine or defecating, as lions and tigers do.*

If cat meets cat in an unmarked area, the encounter will generally be peaceful. But if a stranger intrudes on your cat's personal territory, she will usually see him off in accordance with a fairly rigid set of responses.

First comes the Stare. Cats hate being stared at, which they interpret, rightly in this case, as indicative of aggression. If the Stare doesn't work, or doesn't work quickly enough, the defending cat will move on to the Hiss, a commonplace piece of cat vocabulary that means, in various contexts, *Behave yourself*; *Leave me alone*; *Don't eat my food*; or *Go away*. It's been suggested that hissing by cats is a particularly clever evolutionary development that mimics the warning sound made by a venomous snake and thus makes the cat seem far more dangerous than it actually is. If hissing fails, your cat will next resort to growling, a more serious sound altogether and one that signals, *If you don't go away, I shall attack you*. This is followed shortly afterwards by

---

* I'm told you can get rid of stray cats, dogs and just about any other pest smaller than a gorilla by spreading lion dung obtained from your local zoo.

the caterwaul, an ugly, eerie sound that translates as *I'm warning you, seriously now, that if you don't get off my property at once, I shall do you grievous bodily harm.* To which the intruding cat typically caterwauls back, *Oh, yeah? You and whose army?*

The initial stages can take quite a long time to complete, so that the caterwaul can come as something of a surprise, particularly when the encounter may be broken off at any time by the retreat of either cat. Where nobody retreats, the final stage is a sharp, fast, noisy, ultra-violent attack, sometimes occasioned by the intruder but more often a pre-emptive strike by the defence.

The fight that ensues is characterised by much sound and fury with impressive screams and howls of pain, but generally does not last long and seldom results in serious injury. (Although I should add the caveat that viral leukaemia, a deadly disease, can be passed from cat to cat in what appears to be an insignificant bite.) The exception to this rule is an encounter between two unneutered toms. I once took in a battle-scarred veteran, whose body and head were covered with ancient wounds and whose right ear was two thirds missing.

Your cat learns martial arts as a kitten in violently energetic play fights with siblings or her mother. These are so realistic, accompanied as they are by heart-rending, high-decibel protests of apparently agonising pain, that my soft-hearted wife invariably attempts to break them up. In this, she is doing them no favours for it is in the nature of cats to fight for their territory, and the sooner they learn how to do so, with minimal damage to themselves and their enemies, the better.

The hideous American crone who announced to me smugly that she was having her cat declawed 'to save the furniture' was doing her unfortunate pet no favours either. Cats come equipped at birth with claws, five on their front paws, four on the back. All but the dew claws (on the front) are retractable. All are needed for more than destroying the furniture.

When not in use, your cat's claws are kept sheathed between the pads of her feet. This allows her to walk silently and keeps the claws sharp. But when she needs them, she needs them; and she needs them for hunting, self-defence, climbing trees and extra traction on difficult surfaces. Unfortunately, she learned as a kitten that kneading her mother's belly – tiny claws extended – usually produced a comforting supply of milk. So now, when she seeks comfort on your lap, old habits die hard and kneading begins again – large claws extended – to ruin your best dress or suit. Protest though you may, she will respond only by purring. Comfort yourself by reading advertisements for scratching posts, although my experience is that no cats will actually use them when there is valuable furniture about.

It pains me to be the one to break this to you, but there's an 80 per cent chance your cat may be an incipient junkie. She's unlikely to be sniffing coke or smoking crack, but you need to be wary of nepetalactone, a substance so appealing that she can detect it in a dilution of one part per billion. Where she's most likely to detect it is in plants like catnip, silver vine and valerian. If there are any growing in your garden, your cat will alert you by rolling on them, chewing them and rubbing against them, trilling ecstatically. But, really, there is no need to worry. This behaviour, even by a single cat, will quickly kill off the plant, so the addiction tends to be self-limiting.

If your cat doesn't get high on catnip, she will surely get high by climbing, especially in her younger years. This seems to be an instinct dating back to the time of her wildcat evolution. You can see potential prey at far greater distance if you're perched at the top of a tree; and it's great fun to ambush him by dropping down when he walks underneath. Unfortunately, there is a worrying downside to this behaviour. Cats are excellent climbers, sure-footed and agile, when they are going up, but absolute rubbish when they are coming down. The reason is that they climb using their claws, and their claws face backwards. This simple anatomical fact means your cat can climb a tree as nimbly as a spider, but has to come down backwards in short, ungainly jumps. Before learning this trick, a cat can sometimes find herself crouched on a high perch in need of rescue.

The worry, of course, is that she will fall, but if she does, she is more likely to survive than you would in similar circumstances. Part of the reason is your cat's remarkable agility and the speed of feline thought in grabbing for branches or other protrusions that might break her fall. Another part is the body-twisting reflex that allows cats to land on their feet from any fall greater than about a yard.

There are, however, other threats to your cat's well-being than falling from trees. Worms and fleas, often picked up from prey, are a constant problem. You are well advised to suspect worms if the condition of your cat's coat deteriorates, she develops a dry cough and her appetite increases. Usually a strong appetite is a sign of good health, but worms deprive your cat of nourishment, leaving her perpetually hungry as she tries to compensate. A ravenous appetite combined with weight loss is a strong indicator of worms. Fleas are less easy to diagnose, but patches of granular skin, particularly along the spine, can be a pointer if you don't see the little blood-suckers themselves. Fortunately there are very successful veterinary treatments for both fleas and worms, available as 'spot-on' medications that allow you to avoid the nightmare of trying to feed a cat a pill.

More serious problems, some of them life-threatening, will occasionally come your cat's way, but try not to be too worried as you call the vet. Cats cope with illness by withdrawing into a listless, sometimes almost comatose state. This can easily give the impression they are closer to death than is actually the case. As a result, their subsequent recovery seems little short of a miracle, which, I suspect, gave rise to the old nine-lives belief.

The good news is that, despite disease and fleas and falls from trees, your cat's life expectancy has been quietly getting longer over recent years. I can remember back in the seventies you were lucky to find a cat that lasted much beyond the age of seven. By 1995, for reasons I haven't been able to fathom, life expectancy had risen to almost nine and a half. Today, the average life span is somewhere between twelve and fifteen. My darling goggle-eyed Diddler, who lived on a diet of rabbits when she was younger, died at the age of twenty-one, and I once saw an enormous cat asleep before an open fire whose owner swore was thirty-six. The oldest verified age for a cat, I am reliably informed, is thirty-eight.

You can increase your cat's chances of a ripe old age by neutering. Neutered toms live (on average) nearly twice as long as their intact cousins. Neutered queens don't have such an extreme advantage, but do live more than half as long.

At the other end of the age spectrum, if you acquired your cat as a female kitten and thought you had all the time in the world to have her spayed, the chances are she will astonish you by getting pregnant. Cats can have kittens while they are still kittens themselves – as young as four months – and if you leave them to it, they can have a *lot* of kittens. Given two or three litters a year and a breeding span of roughly ten years, an average queen will present you with about 150 young over her lifetime. If she's above average, the score may be substantially higher. According to *Guinness World Records*, the world's most prolific cat, a tabby from Texas named Dusty, gave birth to 420 kittens.[*]

The trouble starts in spring when a young queen's fancy definitely turns to love. From then until late autumn, she will come into a restless, noisy, howling and noticeably affectionate heat every two weeks for four to seven days. The noise she makes will attract every tom cat in the neighbourhood and fights will ensue with, in true Darwinian fashion, the winner earning the right to mate. In a ritual reminiscent of my teenage years, the queen will reject him time and again before eventually assuming what is known as the lordosis position[†] with her bottom raised and tail tucked tantalisingly out of the way. The tom interprets this, quite correctly, as a come-on. He grips her firmly by the scruff of the neck to stop her wandering off – triggering the same reflex a mother cat uses to paralyse her kittens when she wants to carry them – then mounts her so that mating can take place.

From a human perspective, the act itself is disappointingly short and its conclusion painful for the female. A tom cat's penis is equipped with up to 150 backwards-pointing spines designed to stimulate ovulation by raking the inner walls of the vagina to howls of protest from the queen as her mate dismounts.

[*] http://www.guinnessworldrecords.com/world-records/most-prolific-cat Accessed July 2016.
[†] Neutered males will sometimes adopt this position as well, probably as a signal of submission in a conflict situation.

But the story isn't necessarily over. After mating, your queen will wash herself thoroughly and during this time will refuse, even attack, any tom who dares to come near her. When she has finished, however, in no more than half an hour, she is ready to present herself to another persistent male. Furthermore, her internal anatomy is such that *both* toms can fertilise her so that kittens in the same litter may have different fathers. If ovulation is successfully triggered, the kittens – usually three to five of them – will make their appearance about sixty-six days later. Your cat will look after them well without any interference from you, but guard against visiting toms at this stage. They will often try to kill the kittens in order to bring their mother back on heat.

This then is the biological profile of the world's most popular pet; and, unless I'm missing something, there is nothing in it to explain their special place in our hearts. Nor does it cast much light on several other, perhaps even deeper, mysteries surrounding our feline friends. But we have to start somewhere. Besides which, the profile is incomplete, for it has yet to examine an aspect of cats that is far more important than their average size or hunting habits: their personal stories. This is an oversight we will correct in our next chapter.

Personality Cat

During a turbulent period of my life, I moved into a small country cottage on the outskirts of a sleepy Irish town. At the end of a long day transporting my belongings, I stepped out of my car to be greeted by an urgent miaow. There was no cat in sight, but the sound was close at hand so I called, 'Hello?' and out of a nearby hedgerow strode a sturdy black-and-white kitten. He made a beeline for the front door, sat down, washed himself and waited. It didn't take a genius to figure out what he wanted. I'd been adopted by a little tom cat.

This was my introduction to The Maggot. I subsequently discovered he'd been born into a local family, both of children and cats, who lived only half a mile up the road. To judge by the family's other pets, he'd been well treated, well fed and well loved as a kitten, but some cats just hate crowds and this one clearly preferred the company of a solitary man. I installed a cat flap and The Maggot moved in.

He saw me through a great many emotional ups and downs, mainly by reminding me there were better things to worry about than the vicissitudes of human relationships. In return, I composed a song in his honour, the lyrics of which went:

> Oh, Maggoty-Mookin,
> How do you do-kin?
> Have you been out assaulting mice today?
> Oh, Maggoty-Mookin,
> You're turning quite blue-kin.
> Is that because it's cold outside todaaaaay?

I blush to confess I never had The Maggot neutered, despite constant pressure from his vet, a brilliant, kind and caring lady named Noreen. 'You do realise you won't lose any of your own bits during the operation?' she asked me, during one of our many conversations on the subject. I smiled wanly, but declined to respond. The truth was, her implication was correct: I did have a serious psychological problem when it came to fixing The Maggot. In principle, I was all for it. I knew the world had far too many kittens. But somehow I could not bear the thought of castrating someone who was, at that time, my only close male friend. It seemed such a betrayal.

I excused my decision on the grounds that The Maggot was not like any other tom cat. He was affectionate. He was spotlessly clean. He stayed close to home. He never once sprayed inside the house to mark his territory. He was a big cat and saw off intruding toms with a noisy show of strength rather than actual violence. Besides, a secretly antisocial part of me whispered, he was a *tom* cat. If he ever did produce kittens, they would be somebody else's responsibility, not mine.

The turbulence in my life died down eventually, as turbulence often does. I proposed to Jacks, she accepted, and we set about searching for a home better suited to joint needs than my little Irish cottage or her single-bedroom London flat. An old rectory seemed ideal. Both of us worried about how The Maggot – by now an adult with an established territory – would take the move, but in the event he took it better than we did. He made a thorough inspection of every room, graciously accepted a small snack in his personal bowl, then laid claim to the only sofa we'd so far managed to move in, curled up and went to sleep.

A year later, he brought home a wife and four kittens.

I was in the kitchen when it happened. The Maggot crashed noisily through the cat flap, miaowed in my general direction, then crashed out again. Seconds later he repeated the whole performance. 'What's the matter, Maggot?' I asked. Our next chapter is on the subtleties of cat communication, but there was nothing subtle about this behaviour. The Maggot wanted me to follow him.

The back door from our kitchen led into a gravelled yard with a large double gate opening onto a patch of overgrown wasteland. The Maggot was in the middle of the yard, anxiously looking back to make sure I was following. I could see nothing amiss: no rodent corpses, no dead birds, nothing to explain his odd behaviour. He walked to the gate and trilled. Out of the rough grass in the wasteland walked a long-haired black queen cat. Behind her, in single file, trooped four adorable kittens. One was jet black and long-haired, like the mother. There was no doubting the father of the others: they were all three the spitting image of The Maggot.

The Maggot led them proudly to the back door and waited for me to open it. (Later he trained them all in the use of the cat flap.) When I did so, he marched them inside, direct to the cat-food cupboard, and looked at me expectantly.

The sequence of events I have just described is, of course, impossible – at least, according to conventional wisdom. Consult the most authoritative sources and you will be told the father of kittens plays no part in their upbringing, shows no interest in their welfare and will even murder them all, given half a chance, for the sake of another brief sexual encounter with their mother. But nobody had told The Maggot that. He had clearly decided his mate and kittens deserved something better than a winter in the long grass and led them to warmth, nourishment and safety, having first alerted the human who would provide all three.

Just as you need only one white crow to prove all crows aren't black, so you need only one Maggot to show that the stereotypical idea of cats is nonsense. I would venture to say that while all cats manifest some aspects of the stereotype, no cat manifests them all, and some cats manifest so few that we can scarcely think of them as cats at all. Take another of my cats, the Wobber, who staked his claim to a unique personality while he was still a tiny kitten.

Wobber's mother-to-be, Broccoli Cat One, walked in through our garden door one fine spring afternoon. She was well fed, well groomed and well pregnant, a diminutive tabby with white patches and a pretty face. She subsequently proved to be one of the few cats I've ever known who actually liked small children and didn't mind being carried about like a stuffed toy. She also proved to have a serious foot fetish and would chew the toes of anyone foolish enough to go barefoot in her presence. Jacks fell for her at once and offered her food, which she accepted with a silent miaow. They went off together to find a suitable bed and settled on a cardboard box that once contained a vegetable delivery. The words *broccoli: cat. 1* were scrawled on the outside in black marker.

Three weeks later, Broccoli had her kittens while reclining on Jacks's lap. There were four of them as I recall. We moved mother and kitts into the cardboard box and switched on a radiator to keep them warm at night. Broccoli purred her approval.

Just after the kittens opened their eyes, disaster struck.

Jacks and I came down one morning to a scene of carnage. The cardboard box had been upended. There were vicious scratch marks down one side and the cushion we'd put inside was shredded. Broccoli was cowering in a corner. Frightened squeaks told us her kittens were hiding behind her. All except one. Lying in a pool of blood in the middle of the floor was the corpse of a tiny tiger. 'Oh, no!' Jacks gasped.

The kitten was obviously dead but I went across to make sure. Its mouth was open, its eyes were closed and there was a substantial amount of blood, but I thought I caught the slightest rise and fall of the chest. 'I think it's still alive,' I told Jacks. A voice inside my head whispered, 'But not for long.'

We rang the vet at once. She told us to bring the dying kitten along with its mother and the rest of the brood so that Broccoli would not reject it after an absence if it managed to survive. The vet's surgery was fifty minutes' drive away. The dying kitten was still breathing when we got there . . . And still breathing the following day when we rang to check on his progress. By the end of the afternoon, he was happily feeding again. 'It's looking hopeful,' the vet said. 'But he's been badly injured and may be permanently disabled.'

From the nature of the injury and her past experience, the vet pieced together what had happened. And what had happened was again impossible, according to conventional wisdom. An adult tom cat, hungry for sex, had let himself in through the cat flap and tracked down Broccoli in her cardboard box. His instinct would have been to kill the kittens in order to bring her back on heat. But he never got the chance. While his siblings hid behind their mother, one tiny kitten, only weeks old, attacked the tom cat.

It was an uneven battle, hardly a battle at all in fact. We know the tom cat must have retreated, perhaps astonished by the confrontation, since none of the others was injured. But before he did so, reflex drove him to deliver the bite to the neck that all cats use to kill their prey. The little tiger kitten should have died at once, but miraculously did not. Despite the vet's earliest misgivings, his only permanent damage was to a tendon that left him carrying his head cocked to one side for the rest of his life. This earned him the name Head Wobbler, Wobber for short, and he wore it with pride, a heroic kitten and personality cat.

Some cats have big personalities – Puss in Boots by Gustav Dore

But The Maggot and Wobber were not the only cats of my acquaintance to exhibit distinctive personality traits sometimes bordering on the miraculous. Perhaps the most astounding example of all was the Toxic Moose.

The Toxic Moose was a small, standoffish, neutered queen, who gained one part of her name from her habit of sticking her head through the cat flap, then resting it there so that she looked like a trophy mounted on a wall. The second part of her name arose from the time she bit me and the wound turned septic – the first time any cat has ever managed this. Toxic clearly carried a load of bacteria on her teeth that would have done justice to a Komodo Dragon. She was a little black and white monster, semi-feral, who tolerated Jacks, myself and the other cats purely for the sake of the available food and shelter our home provided on rainy days.

One morning, Jacks found a dead rodent on the inside of the cat flap. Small presents like this are familiar to most cat-owners. One theory is that our pets are trying to teach us how to hunt. Since Jacks had no desire to become a mouser, she picked up the corpse with a view to disposal and it hissed at her.

On closer inspection, the 'dead rodent' turned out to be a newborn kitten, its eyes still closed. Its arrival was bewildering. There was no way it could have climbed through the cat flap on its own, no sign of a mother cat or any siblings. The only thing we could think of was that one of our own cats – we had quite a few at the time – had carried it through the cat flap and left it prominently for us to find. But the theory raised more questions than it answered. Where had the kitten come from? Where were the mother and the rest of the litter? Why had one of our cats decided to kidnap a strange kitten? Why bring it home? Why had the mother cat not protected her offspring? Or was the whole thing a rescue operation?

But the most important question of all was the one Jacks posed when she showed me the little bundle of fur wriggling in the palm of her hand: 'What are we going to do with this?'

The truth was I had not the least idea. The closed eyes suggested the kitten was less than a week old, far too young for solid food, far too young for anything other than mother's milk. 'Maybe it would take cow's milk from a dropper,' I suggested uncertainly.

'I'll heat some,' Jacks said.

We cleaned up an old eyedropper and tried to feed the kitten. Most of the milk went down its chin. After a while, a tiny tongue poked out and a drop or two went in, but it was obvious that dropper-feeding would not provide nearly enough nourishment to ensure the kitten's survival.

We made up a bed in a basket, set it in a warm place and left the kitten to its own devices while we phoned our favourite vet for advice. She suggested we continue with the dropper-feeding, but didn't hold out much hope because of the age of the kitten. 'What it really needs is its mother,' she said.

We went back to the basket. In it was a purring Toxic Moose, happily feeding our latest acquisition.

The Toxic Moose had been spayed three years earlier. There was no question of pregnancy, no way she could lactate on demand. Yet Toxic saw a newborn kitten and produced milk at once. The kitten, eyes still closed, accepted her as a surrogate mother with no problem whatsoever.

Thus began the story of the Diddler, whose birth was a mystery, whose survival was a miracle and who lived with us for twenty-one years.

As unique in her own way as the Diddler was Creepy Krong, a friendly, happy tabby who lived with us in apparent contentment from kittenhood for several years until she disappeared one summer's morning. Even the best-fed cats will sometimes wander off for days at a time, but after a week without Creepy, we began to feel seriously worried and sent out search parties, circulated missing-cat posters and checked with the local cat rescue, as seriously worried owners tend to do. All in vain. We posted a reward in the local paper, but nobody came forward with our missing Creepy. Neither did Creepy turn up on her own. By the time a month had gone by, we were growing resigned to our loss. Creepy had either found a new home or been killed on the road.

Five years later, I came downstairs on Christmas morning and headed for the kitchen for a wake-up cup of coffee. Creepy Krong greeted me with a cheerful miaow from the kitchen table. She was well fed and healthy, perfectly contented to be back in her old home. She took her place with the rest of the cats as if she'd never left. We celebrated Christmas with a champagne toast to the Prodigal Daughter and watched through the coming days as Creepy settled in more and more comfortably.

Three weeks later she disappeared again. I haven't seen her since.

These stories – and there are many like them – ably demonstrate the varying characteristics of individual cats. Some of those characteristics are appealing, some not, but all have one thing in common: they are specific to a particular cat. Which may explain why we respect, like or even love the individual, but provides no clues to the mystery of our relationship with cats in general. For that, we clearly need to expand our understanding of the species as a whole.

Communicating Cat

You can add immensely to your understanding of your cat by learning his language, then watching for examples of its use. You'll notice I said 'watching for' not 'listening to'. Many of a cat's communication skills are non-verbal and most are vested in his fur and tail.

When a kitten is born, he comes complete with a linkage between each and every fur follicle and his automatic nervous system. This linkage is an evolutionary development designed to frighten off enemies. When faced with danger, a kitten's entire covering of fur stands on end, making him look larger and more threatening than he really is. In an adult cat, this reaction takes place only along the spine and tail, but kittens go the whole hog, presumably because they're little and feel they need to.

The response is entirely instinctive, as is the decision of a grown cat to turn sideways, thus giving an enemy the full effect. Your cat's big cousin, the lion, adopts a different strategy, turning face on to show off his mighty mane. The result is the same in both cases: the cat looks larger than he actually is.

We've already noted that you can say a lot with fur, especially if you combine it with a spit or a hiss. Take your pick from the following translations, guided by the context in which the fur rises.

Keep off.
I'm dangerous.
I'm too big for you.
I'm ready to fight.
Retreat if you know what's good for you.
I am likely to attack you at any moment.

You can say a lot with a tail as well. Some experts have it that a cat's tail evolved as an aid to balance, particularly during the process by which felines exercise their well-known ability to fall on their feet. This seemed to be borne out by Kritten Krong (brother of Creepy), who was born without a tail and proved capable of falling off a plank that was lying on the ground. But the latest research indicates that cats use their flexible spines to pull off the balance trick, their tails having little to do with it. In fact, the tail is largely a social appendage and the basis of much cat communication.

It's possible to see the development of tail language from a very early age. Watch any young kitten run enthusiastically towards its mother. The tail will be upright and ramrod straight except for a short length at the tip, which waves about freely like a semaphore flag. And semaphore – or something akin – is what is

actually going on, with the kitten signalling variations
on the following themes:

Hello, Mum.
Any milk on the go?
It's lovely to see you.
I'm ever so happy.
Let's snuggle.
All is well with the world.

The mother cat will typically respond with a soft,
pleasing, whirring sound, which means, *Hello, my lovely:
nice to see you too*. (But if a cat honours *you* with a whir,
it's usually a thank-you for some small service, like
opening a door.)

As kittens grow older, their tail language grows more
complex. The simple tail-up undergoes subtle changes
and is often joined by other signs. From a greeting
originally reserved for its mother, the cat replaces the
waving tip with a small hook and uses it to greet familiar human companions. Translation into English
becomes more complex as well.

Without the hook, the upright tail means simply *hello*.

With the hook, this signal is *hello, I'm happy to see you*.
Combined with an ankle polish, we have the message,
*It's good to see you because I'm hungry. I hereby mark you as
my own. Are you ready to serve me? Some food would be nice.
Here, let me show you my empty dish* . . . At which point, the
cat abandons his ankle polishing and trots off – tail still

erect – to the feeding area, casting brief glances over his shoulder to make sure you're following.

If there is no food in the bowl, your cat will sit down beside it, looking up at you expectantly. Should you fail to fill it quickly enough, your cat will encourage you with a verbal miaow. (Translation: *Get a move on. Can't you see I'm starving to death down here?*)

If the bowl already contains food, the cat will approach enthusiastically, tail up, but will not begin to eat before making a thorough inspection. This he does using his nose and a second olfactory organ in the roof of his mouth. Between them, they give him a sense of smell that is vastly better than ours and arguably even better than that of a dog. As a result, he uses scent rather than sight as his primary way of exploring the world and is well able to detect toxins in food that we might easily miss, even on close inspection. Assuming the food passes muster, he will begin to eat. As he does so, he will allow his tail to arc slowly downwards until it is flat on the floor stretched out straight behind him. (Translation: *This meal is acceptable. Don't disturb me until I've finished. Oh, and be careful not to tread on my tail.*) Should the food fail to pass muster, however, your cat will engage in one of the most vivid pieces of playacting you are ever likely to see in the animal kingdom. Turning his back on the bowl, he will begin to scratch imaginary earth over the food. (Translation: *You are feeding me shit.*)

When a cat heads towards you with her tail hooked to one side, you may be (fairly) sure you are about to experience a small show of affection. Typically what she will do is walk directly past you without any apparent acknowledgement. But in the process she will allow her tail to curl briefly around your calf, giving it the smallest stroke as she continues on her way. This is often done under a table, so that by the time you check to find out who's rubbing your leg, the cat has long gone. The gesture translates as *I like you* or, more rarely when it's a strange cat, *I'd like to get to know you better*. Basically, it's the feline equivalent of flirting, but don't expect too much in the way of follow-through: a cat will always play hard to get.

When a cat's tail is erect and fluffed, there are several possible translations. One, seen with cats on the run, is *I am being pursued by a deadly enemy*. Another may be *I've just been badly startled*. Where there is another cat in the vicinity, the likely meaning is *I'm upset* or *I'm upset and angry and planning an imminent attack*. A rigidly straight tail, fluffed from root to tip, is a direct threat. Raised but arched forward indicates a cat on the defensive whereas an inverted U can be taken as a sign of anxiety – usually only seen in a cat that is being chased. Lashing the tail violently, whether bushed or not, is a sign of extreme anger and will often precede physical violence. An exception to this rule arises when two cats are playing together. Here the lashing of a tail means *I am pretending to be extremely angry*. Once again physical violence is likely to follow, but all in fun.

Sometimes an elevated tail is combined with other, different, examples of cat communication. While lions are often referred to as the only social cat because they hunt in packs, house cats that manage to live together harmoniously will typically bond together to form a mutually supportive collective. Often unknown to their owners, any established group of this sort will set up a sophisticated security system to protect their home from being infiltrated by intruders, just as a large company might protect its offices by installing combination locks on the doors and issuing pass codes only to legitimate visitors. With cat groups, however, a closer analogy would be those ultramodern systems that depend on fingerprint or iris recognition.

Any cat approaching a well-established group would be strongly advised to do so with tail erect and fur smooth, signalling *I come in peace*. But once contact is made with a fellow feline, the equivalent of an iris-recognition system swings into operation, except that rather than looking the cat in the eye, a security officer examines a visitor's credentials by looking it in the bottom.

Compared to humans, cats are notably short-sighted and rely on their sense of smell – which, remember, is probably keener than that of a dog – as an aid to recognition. To facilitate the process, the visiting cat will present its bottom, tail modestly raised, for inspection. Anal scent glands establish its personal identity as securely as the prints on the tips of your fingers. Overall, the translation is, *Examine my credentials. You'll find I'm harmless/an old friend.*

Cats' spoken language is far from simple. Although not often realised, a hearty miaow is among the vocalisations possible for big cats, like lions and tigers, presumably used as some form of cat-to-cat communication. But while domestic cats miaow far more often than any lion, they seem to reserve this type of communication almost entirely for humans. Which leads me to speculate that some, and quite possibly a great deal of, cat behaviour may have evolved directly from their contact with humans. Certainly some of them have seemed to pick up humanlike characteristics – I once had a cat who taught herself to open doors. (She jumped up and swung on the handles, then sauntered through.) Gaze into your cat's eyes and you will find yourself in contact with a consciousness that is at once quite alien, yet strangely familiar, and, in many ways, close to your own. These are all points we shall return to, at a substantially deeper level, later in this book. For now, we can confine ourselves only to the more superficial aspects of cat communication.

But superficial or not, tail signals combine with a whole variety of other signs to create conversations of considerable complexity. The positioning of the cat's body will modify a tail signal, as will the placement of whiskers, the flattening of ears against the head, dilation of the pupils and a variety of howls, hisses and other sounds. Some recent scientific research suggests a cat's miaow can be tailored in pitch to mimic sounds made by human babies, thus guaranteeing immediate attention. As mentioned before, experts also speculate that the combination of flattened ears, bared fangs and especially hissing – seen when a cat is threatened – is designed to mimic the behaviour of a snake, sending a clear message that *I may be small, but I am deadly.*[*]

A cat will never ignore a visiting feline, although he will sometimes pretend to do so. He may scan the sky, wash fur on his shoulder, yawn and even close his eyes to slits with every sign of total relaxation. But it all amounts to one big bluff. Let the other cat make a move and he is instantly alert, quite possibly bushed up ready for battle.

Scent also forms an important part of feline communication. Urine traces, no more than a bad smell to you and me, carry much more information to your cat. How long ago was the trace laid down? Was it placed by a tom or a queen? Was he/she sexually aroused? Above all, does this trace signal impending danger? Sometimes the urine trace will be combined with some other sign. Domestic tom cats will frequently reach up on their hind legs to scratch bark on the trunk of a tree before turning to spray it with their urine. This is a trick our pets have somehow picked up from their cousins the big cats, who do exactly the same thing in

[*] http://www.stumbleupon.com/su/1v1u8y/:o9of@fqb:CCa!O1c!/ www.cracked.com/article/226_6-adorable-cat-behaviors-with-shockingly-evil-explanations_p1 Accessed September 2016.

the wild. In both cases, the message is the same: *Beware, a very big cat lives here.*

Although learning the language described in this chapter would be of obvious benefit to humans, most of it evolved for use cat to cat. When a cat wants to communicate with a human she sometimes resorts to charades, as The Maggot did when he wanted to introduce me to his wife and children. But developing a specific charade cannot be dismissed as simple instinct. It is a complex intellectual exercise, one we might expect to be well beyond the capacity of a cat. How The Maggot and his ilk ever manage it is a profound mystery. And not the only cat communication mystery.

The Secret Communication Channel

At the beginning of April 2015, journalist Sam Bourne reported in an internet blog, the Wet Nose Press, on a new European study that suggested cats had telepathic abilities. Recent experiments carried out at the Sloof Lirpa Institute in Brussels showed that all members of the family *Felidae*, from tigers to tabbies, were capable of low levels of telepathy.

Bourne explained how tests were administered on a number of cat species – ranging from lynxes to lions – at the Planckendael Animal Park outside Brussels. While thinking of a specific thing – like a colour, shape, direction or action – researchers would encourage the cats to stare at them. Sensors were placed on the animals to collect data on their heart rate, blood pressure, body temperature and other vital signs. While things like colours or shapes did not register a definitive reaction, when the researcher thought of a direction or action, 87 per cent of the time the cats would display an appropriate response. If, for example, the researcher thought of running, the cat would tense and become focused, as if ready to give chase. If the researcher thought about sleeping, the cat would relax. Control studies using other animals showed only a one in thirty response to similar stimuli.

The research excited me until the mischievous Sam Bourne admitted his entire report had been an April Fool's Day prank, but there are still patterns of domestic feline behaviour I am hard put to explain without evoking the theory of telepathy.

I have two close friends who have serious problems with cats. One – I'll call her Marion to preserve her privacy – suffers from a phobia that at one time rendered her unable to remain in the same room as a cat. The other, Fintan, has an allergy so severe that to brush against a cat, or even somewhere a cat has been sitting, leaves him ill for weeks. Obviously, they both avoid cats wherever possible, but the reverse is far from true. When they visit the feline-infested rectory that is my home, they instantly become cat magnets. Cats that normally run and hide at the approach of visitors will emerge from the woodwork to sit at the feet of these two guests, staring malevolently. Cats who are usually coldly aloof to all human contact will try desperately to climb on their knees, purring insanely.

This is an extreme example of the pattern and another mystery, but I have observed a much more common version of it, not only among my own cats but in many other households. Why do cats tend to gravitate towards people who dislike them? Those who adore cats, by contrast, are treated with high levels of disdain. And the question wrapped up in the mystery is: how do the cats know who likes them and who doesn't?

Sometimes, of course, the answer is obvious, with the clue in the human's behaviour. It's not difficult to spot the cat-lover who pats her lap and calls, 'Here, puss.' But how does the cat segregate those who exhibit no such signs? I began to suspect telepathy when I noticed another behaviour pattern among my own cats.

Like most cat-minders, I invariably find myself with one cat who prefers my lap above all others. This is not to say she sits on me all the time, but when she fancies a lap, it is mine she chooses. Deaths in the feline family have meant the identity of this cat has changed from time to time, but one thing has remained constant: sooner or later, each one has developed a curious ability to sense when I have decided to get up from my chair.

There would be little mystery about this ability if it manifested while the cat was on my lap – changes in posture or unconscious muscle movements on my part would provide a rational explanation – but it typically arises on those rare times I have an empty lap. The sequence of events goes like this:

I am sitting catless in an armchair.

My cat is seated or lying (sometimes apparently asleep) on a mat, couch or other favourite location.

It occurs to me I would like a gin and tonic (with ice and lemon) and decide to get up and make one.

The cat at once moves from its current position and jumps onto my lap.

She makes herself comfortable, curls up and purrs.

I settle back and mentally wave my gin goodbye. I have been, in a word coined by a British cat-owner recently, incapussitated.

This sequence has occurred literally scores of times during my life. It is as if my cat somehow knew about my intent to stand up and decided she wanted to sit on my lap instead. Since, as often as not, she isn't even looking in my direction – and occasionally is not even in the same room – when I make my initial decision, I can think of no explanation for her trick other than telepathy.

But, then, I am not the only one to gather evidence that domestic cats sometimes exhibit a talent for mind-reading. The American author Barbara Holland tells* a fascinating story about a semi-feral tom cat she named Boston Blackie. Holland and her family were serious cat-lovers, with thirteen house cats of their own and a

* Barbara Holland, *Secrets of the Cat: its Lore, Legend and Lives*, HarperCollins (Kindle edition), 2010.

penchant for feeding any an
up on their doorstep. They lov
But Boston Blackie proved hard t

Blackie was a thug. He was wa
positively hated other cats. In fact, he se
mission to kill every feline on the planet.   cked
those of the Holland household viciously and   quently,
without the slightest provocation. While he failed – if
only just – to kill any of them, he typically left them so
mauled and mutilated that veterinary attention was
needed.

As the vet bills mounted, and more and more time
was taken up with nursing Blackie's victims, the Holland
family realised they had a serious problem on their
hands. As cat-lovers often do, they tried to solve it by
throwing food into the bushes for Blackie. It made no
difference to his murderous ways.

Sterner measures were clearly needed and the family
decided to try to trap him, with the idea of taking him
far, far away. Despite baiting the cage with various cat
treats, Blackie ignored it . . . and continued to attack the
Holland pets.

A family conference seriously considered poison, but
dismissed the idea because of the risk to their own
animals. In soul-searching desperation, they finally
decided to ask a friend who owned a gun to come and
shoot the outlaw. Arrangements were made for Blackie's
execution on the evening of the day that Barbara
Holland returned from a short holiday.

arrived back on Tuesday afternoon, just hours before the deed was to be done. She began the routine of feeding her own cats. As she did so, Blackie emerged from the bushes, strolled across the lawn and demanded food – in his own dish. When a bewildered Barbara fed him, he picked a sunny spot on the porch and lay down to sleep, ignoring the wary menagerie of house cats all around him. Then he moved in and, from that point on, became a house cat. He never attacked another cat.

There was considerable speculation about this astonishing change of behaviour. Theories ranged from a tumour on the brain to simple madness. Eventually the family decided on what they called their 'cartoon solution': Blackie had been a peaceful house cat who received a blow on the head, causing him to lose his memory. After a period in the wilderness, a second blow to the head caused him to remember his real character.

A theory they did not consider was what some might argue to be the most obvious of all: Blackie was telepathic. He picked up on the plan for his impending execution from the minds of family members, just in time to change his wanton ways.

If Boston Blackie was indeed telepathic, there are strong suggestions he is not the only cat to exhibit this useful power. They come from a new breed of 'animal communicators' typified by a widely publicised British practitioner named Pea Horsley.

Cat-lover Pea had been working for fifteen years as a theatre stage manager in London when a meeting with a dog changed her life. Pea was on a visit to the Mayhew Animal Home in Trenmar Gardens when she fell in love with a mongrel called Morgan.

It was an unlikely development. Pea had been afraid of dogs since she was chased by a pack of Jack Russells as a girl. But there was something special about Morgan and, almost before she knew it, she'd signed the adoption papers and was taking him home to meet her current cat, Texas. Although Texas was not best pleased to have a canine companion, the two animals settled well enough, but Morgan seemed sad and exhibited several puzzling behavioural characteristics. Sensitive to her lack of experience with dogs, Pea readily accepted an emailed invitation from the Mayhew Home to attend an animal communication workshop with the promise of getting to know her pet better.

For most people, animal communication is learning the signs an animal displays while experiencing a particular emotion, as when a cat purrs to express contentment or bushes up its fur in anticipation of a fight. But if Pea expected to learn the basic canine signals, she was soon to be disappointed.

The day of the workshop, an autumnal Sunday in 2004, rolled around and proved at first an unmitigated disaster. Pea found an uncomfortable plastic chair in a class of twenty and listened with sinking heart while their teacher made the nonsensical claim that he could actually talk to animals and had held conversations with horses since he was a teenager. He spent the morning telling emotional anecdotes about how his miraculous gift had helped the lives of various animals and gave his students one or two sensitivity exercises, which involved no work with animals at all. By lunch time, Pea was all but ready to go home.

In the afternoon, things livened up a little. The class members were split up into pairs and instructed to swap photographs of the pet they had at home – but to do so face down so that the recipient had no idea what the pet was. The teacher then instructed them to try to guess the animal in the picture. A cynical Pea angrily wrote down the first thing that came into her head: *rabbit*. Then she turned the photo over.

It was a picture of a rabbit.

The term *psychometry* was coined in 1842 by an American professor of physiology named Joseph R. Buchanan. It is drawn from the Greek and means literally 'soul measuring'. In modern psychology, it is used to describe the scientific measurement of certain mental processes. Buchanan, however, was involved in something rather more peculiar.

In a series of experiments, he placed various drugs in glass vials, then asked his students to identify them merely by holding the vials. Their success rate proved higher than chance expectation. Buchanan theorised that all objects have souls that retain a memory of their essence.

After Buchanan published his results, an American professor of geology, William F. Denton, conducted his own experiments to see if psychometry would work with geological specimens. In 1854, he enlisted the help of his sister, Annie Denton Cridge. The professor wrapped his specimens in cloth to avoid any visual clue to their nature. Annie placed the wrapped package to her forehead and discovered she was able to describe the specimens accurately from the vivid mental images she received.

In 1919 the investigation was taken up by Gustav Pagenstecher, a German doctor and psychical researcher, after he discovered psychometric abilities in one of his patients, Maria Reyes de Zierold. While holding an object, Maria could discern facts about the object's past and present, describing sights, sounds, smells and other feelings associated with it.[*]

I was introduced to psychometry by a spiritualist medium when I was in my thirties and discovered I had a talent for it. Like Pagenstecher's Maria, I found that holding an object evoked associated sights, sounds, smells and sometimes even emotions. The technique I learned is sufficiently simple for you to discover in only a few minutes whether you have the knack yourself:

1. Have a friend supply you with a small object you know nothing about. Preferably this should be something that has not been recently immersed in water or chemically cleaned.

***

[*] http://paranormal.about.com/cs/espinformation/a/aa063003.htm

2. Hold the object in contact with your forehead and close your eyes.
3. Relax and report any mental images as they arise. If your friend confirms that the images accurately reflect the history of the object, then you have successfully practised psychometry.

That's the skeleton of the art. I discovered it is helpful to clear the mind at the beginning of a session by allowing images to arise without censorship even though they might be easily guessed (or actually known to you) in relation to the object. Begin by describing the object aloud, followed by anything you already know or might reasonably guess about it. This process acts as a sort of 'priming the pump' and will soon begin to drag up genuine psychometric images.

Meanwhile Pea Horsley's experience at the workshop continued. The facilitator instructed participants to ask the animal a series of questions – What's your favourite food? Where do you like to sleep? and so on. Pea asked them, feeling foolish, and, to her surprise, heard a response like a male voice in her head.* Some of the answers were easily guessed – the rabbit's favourite food was leaves – but others were less readily explained away. Pea was, for example, able to discover that the rabbit's favourite occupation was sitting on a couch watching television and that he was in love with an

---

* The rabbit's owner told her he was male. His name was Mr Butch.

espresso-coloured female. Not all Pea's information was correct but enough of it was to shake her initial cynicism. And the cynicism cracked completely when her workshop partner accurately described Pea's own home, using a photograph of Pea's cat.

Pea went home and fine-tuned her new-found talent by way of telepathic conversations with Morgan. These communications were so successful that she actually came to look on Morgan as a sort of canine mentor. Pea extended her range by offering free consultations to anyone who wanted communication with their pets in return for their verifying the details. At the time, Pea had a back-stage career in London theatre, working with people like playwright Harold Pinter, and actors Alan Rickman and Edward Fox, but as her confidence increased, she resigned the day job and took the enormously courageous step of becoming a professional animal communicator, 'helping people make a telepathic connection with their animals to bring clear, direct understanding and aid healing relationships'.*

It was a risk that paid off. According to her website,† she now has an international practice with clients in Great Britain, France, Spain, Italy, Belgium, Germany, Portugal, Switzerland, Norway, Israel, Panama, Malaysia, South Africa, Korea, Russia, United Arab Emirates, Canada, Japan, United States, New Zealand

---

* Pea Horsley, *Heart to Heart*, Harper Element (Kindle edition), 2013.
† http://www.animalthoughts.com/

and Australia. She no longer has the slightest doubt about her ability to communicate telepathically with a whole range of animal species – including cats – and it is difficult to believe her client list became so impressive if she was unable to get results.

Pea is not the only professional to offer animal-communication services. Even the most superficial trawl of the internet produces a striking list of practitioners, each one advertising talents similar to those described in Pea's book, and using similar methods. Their claims are backed by case studies and testimonials. Among their number is Lori Amato, an American communicator, who believes that anyone can learn to speak with cats given a little basic training. In an article published on the internet, she has this to say:

The best way to start is to go to a quiet room where you will not be distracted. Either have the animal or a picture of a friend's animal with you. Quiet and still yourself . . . close your eyes. When you feel ready, open your eyes and begin to focus on the animal or the animal's picture. Begin to observe the animal [in the picture]. Notice the fur, the body, and the eyes, the breathing. Move deeper if you can . . . say 'hello' to the animal. You may experience . . . a feeling, a vision, a vibration, a voice, a smell . . . The next step is asking a simple question. What is your favorite color? What is your favorite toy? Continue writing down anything you may get in your journal . . .

Where you go from here is entirely up to you. The more you practice you will find that you may be speaking with a cat on a matter of philosophy or perhaps connecting with a beloved pet who has died ... When I first started, I saw pictures or symbols in my head. I had a knowing or a feeling about something at times. At times, I now get actual words, visions, and smells. Animals can communicate on many different levels as we all can.*

So does Sam Bourne's April Fool spoof contain an important truth after all? Are cats (and many other animals) telepathic? Pea Horsley and others use the term freely in their promotional material and, while content may vary, mind to mind contact seems to take place in certain cases. But perhaps not in all. Before deciding finally whether cats are telepathic, it might be sensible to suggest the area warrants some serious scientific investigation. And, fortunately, at least one scientist is prepared to give it.

* https://greytarticles.wordpress.com/behavior-training-22/relation-ships-with/let%E2%80%99s-talk-communicate-telepathically-with-your-pets-4210/

A Scientist's View

Dr Rupert Sheldrake is a British biologist who began his research career working on the development of plants and the ageing of cells. A conventional scientific training left him sceptical about the paranormal, so in his early working days he had little interest in investigating phenomena that he 'knew' to be impossible. But he eventually came to question his own scepticism, and in 1981 he published his first book containing a formulation of his theory of morphic resonance.

In this theory, Sheldrake postulated the existence of a hitherto undetected field phenomenon linking biological entities and providing a medium for possible information transfer between them. As a proposed example of the field in action, he quoted a case study dating back to the days when milk was delivered to British doorsteps each morning in foil-topped glass bottles. The system worked well until a small bird called a tit discovered it could have a drink of cream by pecking a hole in the foil top. Within days, tits across the British Isles were attacking milk bottles for the sake of their cream.

A question naturally arose: how did all the other birds learn the trick? Direct observation had to be ruled out because of the speed with which the knowledge spread and the fact that it proved capable of jumping between areas – like offshore islands – that did not permit direct physical contact.

For Dr Sheldrake, the answer was his postulated morphic field. 'As part of this research, I became interested in the bonds between members of social groups and realised that the morphic fields of a social group could lead to telepathic connections between members of the group. I then investigated telepathy in animals, starting from this biological perspective . . .'

Sheldrake went on to publish more than eighty papers in peer-reviewed journals. About half were on plant development, crop physiology, cell biology and a plant hormone called auxin. The rest, published from the 1980s onwards, were on less reputable subjects like the experimenter effect, the sense of being stared at and telepathy in animals. Among the animals he investigated for signs of telepathy were domestic cats.

The results of his investigations came to public attention in 1999 when he published *Dogs That Know When Their Owners Are Coming Home*. Despite the title, a substantial proportion of the work dealt with feline behaviour. In his opening to the relevant section, Sheldrake remarked bluntly, 'Many cats seem to know when their owners are returning.' And he backed his opinion with some interesting statistics.

Sheldrake revealed that his appeals for information had resulted in no fewer than 359 accounts of what appeared to be telepathic talent in cats. A random survey of some 1,200 households in Britain and America unearthed 91 households with cats that seemed to know when their owner was coming home, some eight per cent of the total.

Analysis of the data produced additional information. About three-quarters of the returns followed relatively short absences – where the owner was coming back from work or school, for example. In 70 per cent of the cases the cat would consistently wait for only one person. In a further 20 per cent, it would wait for either of two people, while cats waiting for three or more people accounted for only 10 per cent of the total. Perhaps predictably, the people cats waited for were those with whom they had a close emotional bond, usually members of the immediate family or very close friends.

In his book, Sheldrake quotes Jeanne Randolph of Washington DC, one of his interview subjects, describing the circumstances of a fairly typical case:

My boyfriend gave me a kitten named Sami for Christmas. Nearly every evening he would stop by my apartment after work. I always knew when he was coming because Sami would sit by the door for approximately ten minutes before his arrival.

I had no way of giving the cat signals because I was never aware of the time he would be coming over. He was in real estate and had erratic hours. I doubt Sami could have heard his car as I live in the middle of very noisy city in a high-rise.

When my mom visits she says Sami anticipates my arrival in the same fashion – and I take the subway.*

In most cases, the cat will start waiting less than ten minutes before the person actually arrives. Again, this naturally raises the suspicion that we may be dealing with nothing more mysterious than the animal's remark-able range of hearing. But Sheldrake dismisses the suggestion: 'Practically all the stories involve behaviour that does not seem explicable in terms of routine, famil-iar sounds, or other straightforward explanations.' As an example, he outlines another of his case studies:

When the teenage son of Dr Carlos Sarasola was living with him in his apartment in Buenos Aires, Argentina, he often came home late at night, after his father had gone to bed with their cat, Lennon. Dr Sarasola noticed that Lennon would suddenly jump off the bed and go and wait by the front door about ten to fifteen minutes before his son arrived, having travelled by taxi.

Intrigued by this behaviour, Dr Sarasola made careful observations of the time the cat responded to

---

* Rupert Sheldrake, *Dogs That Know When Their Owners Are Coming Home*, Cornerstone Digital (Kindle edition), 2013.

see if the cat could be reacting to the sound of the taxi door shutting. It was not, because the cat responded well before the taxi arrived. 'One night I paid attention to several taxis that stopped at the front of my building. Three taxis stopped and Lennon remained quiet with me in bed. Some time later, he jumped down and went to the door. Five minutes later I heard the taxi arrive in which my son was travelling.'[*]

Another case study underlines the point:

My father's cat went down to the front gate and sat on a stone gate post waiting for him about ten minutes before he returned home. As a journalist, his hours were very variable. My mother said that she knew to put the potatoes on when the cat looked up, apparently listened, then trotted off. It can't have been the distant sound of the car, however, because it went even when he had no car and returned by bus and on foot.[†]

Yet another American respondent reported that her cat Minu would growl like a dog for anything up to twenty minutes while she was driving home . . . even when it was an unusual time or a different car.

Cats being cats, it comes as little surprise to note that some only respond to their owner's return when they

[*] *Ibid.*
[†] *Ibid.*

are hungry. Less obvious is that female cats tend to respond most when pregnant, but show notably diminished interest once the kittens arrive. Apart from this understandable anomaly, there was little observable difference between the behaviours of toms and queens.

Does reacting to an owner's return necessarily involve telepathy? One incident, reported by Judith Preston-Jones and her husband, would seem to suggest that it does. The couple were interested in Sheldrake's work and kept a detailed log of the behaviour of their two Siamese cats, Flora and Maia. Like so many other cats, these two consistently reacted to Judith's return after a period of absence. But on one occasion they seemed to get it wrong.

Judith had been attending a church meeting some three miles away from her home in Tonbridge, Kent, and returned at 9.40 p.m. Her husband, who had been observing the cats, told her that they had become restless at 9 p.m., leading him to expect her back by about 9.10 p.m. It seemed as if the cats had made a mistake. But Judith soon convinced him this was not the case. She had in fact left the church at 9 p.m., then remembered there was something she wanted to discuss with a friend and went back in. She remained a further half-hour before setting off again: the cats had reacted to her initial decision, strongly suggesting a direct mind-to-mind contact.

Although the majority of cases Dr Sheldrake studied involved pets, their owners and strong bonds of affection, there were a few exceptions. One of the most interesting involved a Manhattan resident named Mosette Broderick, who volunteered to help a former professor by taking his cat, Kitty, to the vet when she needed medical treatment. Kitty greatly disliked veterinary attention and quickly came to associate it with Mosette – to such an extent that she would run and hide under the stairs of the professor's 62nd Street home whenever Mosette turned onto the same block. She managed the trick although Mosette would typically arrive at entirely random intervals along a busy New York thoroughfare, packed with pedestrians and cars. Since the use of her normal five senses could clearly be ruled out, it seemed Kitty had somehow set up a sort of telepathic radar to detect the approach of her 'enemy'.

Despite the cat's long historical association with the supernatural, Dr Sheldrake's research indicates telepathy may be more widely practised by dogs. The survey of 1,200 households showed over half (55 per cent) of their dogs could regularly anticipate the return of their owners while the figure for cats demonstrating the same talent was a lowly 30 per cent. But, as Sheldrake points out, this does not necessarily mean dogs are better at it. It could simply be that cats don't care as much. In one case study, a woman returned home on a very cold day to find that her cats, who would normally greet her on the doorstep, were curled up on top of the boiler keeping warm.

There are other differences in the telepathic behaviour of cats and dogs. According to the Sheldrake surveys, 17 per cent of dogs will typically react when the owners are setting off to come home, or even when they simply make the decision to come home, before they physically leave. The figure for cats is less than 1 per cent. Many other dogs react only when their owners reach a particularly critical stage of the journey home, like getting off a plane or train. Only 2 per cent of cats show the same pattern. For cats, the crucial time to 'tune in' is typically when their owners are in transit and fairly close.

Dr Sheldrake has also noticed a different response pattern in cats depending on whether the owners have been away for a short or a long time. Where the absence has been short, a cat tends to react only ten to fifteen minutes before the owner arrives home. For longer absences, such as holidays, reaction time is typically measured in hours or even more. Dr Walther Natsch from Herrliberg in Switzerland reports: 'While we were away the animal was with our neighbours. At the moment when we set off in Greece, Turkey or Italy (shorter distances, of course, too) the cat insisted on staying in our house again for the night.'*

Another of Sheldrake's respondents described an even more remarkable example of telepathic ability in a cat. Elisabeth Bienz was forced to leave her cat in the care of

---

* *Ibid.*

her parents when she moved her home from Switzerland to France. But the cat had other ideas and disappeared from her parents' property only days after Elisabeth left. Each time she returned for a visit, however – every two or three months on average – the cat would turn up again, well fed and cared for. When she went back to Paris, he would hang around for a couple of days, then disappear again. On one occasion, he actually turned up just hours in advance of an unannounced visit.

Dr Sheldrake is happy to accept telepathy as a possible – even likely – explanation of his findings. He believes that the evident bonds between cats and their humans involve connections through morphic fields and suggests that these connections are stretched, not broken, when a person goes away and leaves the cat behind. 'The bonds are the channels through which telepathic communication can occur, even over hundreds of miles.'

If such bonds actually exist, operative but largely unrecognised, they may go some way towards explaining why we find cats so irresistible. Humanity has long been drawn towards the mysterious, long been fascinated by any hint of psychism. And if cats really are telepathic, there is evidence to suggest it may not be their only psychic power.

The Precognitive Cat

A few years before the outbreak of the Second World War, a stray cat presented herself to demand sanctuary at St Augustine's and St Faith's Church in Watling Street, London, not far from St Paul's Cathedral. The rector promptly threw her out. The cat came back. The rector threw her out again.

Anyone with experience of feline perseverance could have warned the rector he was playing a mug's game. Father Henry Ross closed the door on her for the third time with a feeling of satisfaction, but he was talking to his verger the following morning when he had the unmistakable feeling of a cat looking at him – and there she was, an adorable little tabby that had, despite the priest's best efforts, somehow managed to spend the night in the warmth and comfort of the church.

The verger, a sensible man named Thomas Evans, volunteered to throw her out again, but Father Ross was in the throes of a conversion. He noticed, apparently for the first time, how thin she looked and wondered aloud if they shouldn't offer her some food.

Mr Evans pointed out that if they started to feed the cat they would never get rid of her. But by this stage the rector was beyond redemption. He decreed that henceforth the cat should stay in his rectory, which abutted the church, at least until somebody claimed her.

Nobody did claim the cat. Eventually Father Ross decreed she should become the official church cat and cemented her position by christening her 'Faith' after one of the two saints to whom the church was dedicated. From that moment on, Faith started to act as if she owned the place, turning up for church services, greeting parishioners, curling up at Father Ross's feet when he gave a sermon . . .

You may be wondering why I'm telling you all this. So far, it sounds like a perfectly predictable example of the way cats go about persuading innocently unsuspecting humans to provide them with food, shelter and a luxury lifestyle. But bear with me. The story is about to take a creepy turn, one with astounding implications.

Outside Faith's cosy little ecclesiastical kingdom, the world moved on and, in September 1939, Great Britain toppled into war with Nazi Germany in response to its invasion of Poland.

At first, nothing much happened. Nobody invaded anywhere else. Nobody dropped a bomb. Nobody fired a single artillery shell. As a result, people began to relax, order another pint and talk about the Phoney War. But the Phoney War lasted only eight months and came to an abrupt end on 10 May 1940, when Germany launched an all-too-successful attack on France and the Netherlands. Three months later, in the comparative quiet of her London church, Faith produced a single kitten. He was a cute little white tom with black ears and tail. Faith's human servants were so taken by him that they posted a birth notice in the church and instructed the choir to sing 'All Things Bright and Beautiful' in his honour.° Because of his colouring, they named him 'Panda'.

On 6 September – and this date is important – Father Ross was working at his desk when Faith began to behave oddly. She stared at the rector, then went to the door of the room and sat waiting until he realised she wanted him to follow her. When he finally did so, she led him downstairs, then stopped at the closed door to the basement and refused to move until he opened it. She then bounded down the steps to explore the cellar. Father Ross went back to his work, leaving the cellar door open so she could get out again.

A little later that day, Faith was spotted carrying her kitten down to the basement.

At first, everybody assumed she'd bring him back up again. But she didn't. She appeared at her regular meal-time (alone), then disappeared. A worried Father Ross headed for the basement to look for her.

The cellar was dank, dark, cold and full of junk, with piles of old books and dusty stacks of sheet music. Faith was curled up with her kitten in a shadowy corner

---

° http://www.purr-n-fur.org.uk/famous/faith.html

between two of these stacks. Under the common delusion that humans know best, Father Ross carried the kitten back upstairs to the warmth of his mother's basket. Faith followed with a barrage of protesting miaows.

But Father Ross wasn't listening. He popped the kitten into the basket, spoke firmly to Faith, then went off to take a church service. When he returned, both kitten and cat were no longer where he'd left them.

By now the good priest was learning a little about cats – notably how stubborn they can be – so he took himself at once to the cellar. Sure enough, there were Faith and Panda curled up together in their dark corner. Determined not to be bested, Father Ross carried Panda straight back to the basket upstairs, once again followed by a protesting Faith. When he went to look in on them

Cats have always been linked with the occult.

the following morning, the basket was empty and cat and kitten were back in the basement.

Stubborn as a cat himself, Father Ross carried the kitten back upstairs again, but by mid-afternoon the basket was empty. At this point, doubtless with feelings of desperation, Father Ross decided to consult the cat-loving wife of his verger, who advised him to let the damn cat have her way and suggested he bring the basket down to the basement so she and her kitten could at least have a bit of comfort. He took the advice, cleared some additional space and left Faith and Panda purring happily in their new home.

That evening, 7 September, Nazi planes began what turned out to be the first of fifty-seven consecutive nights of bombing London – the infamous London Blitz. It was an operation that destroyed or damaged more than a million of the city's houses and killed some twenty thousand of her civilian population. Bombs fell near the church.

On 9 September, Father Ross cycled to Westminster on business. The air-raid warning sirens sounded as he was returning home, forcing him to spend the night in a public shelter. The following morning, a radio broadcast alerted him to the worrying fact that among the casualties of the night before were eight churches. The bulletin did not mention whether St Augustine's and St Faith's was among them. Once the all-clear sounded, Father Ross hurried to find out.

He reached Watling Street to discover the tower of his church still standing, but the remainder a smoking ruin.

Firemen were on the scene. One called a warning for him to keep clear as the roof was about to collapse. Father Ross ignored him and began to clamber over the debris. He knew there were no people in the church overnight, but he feared for the lives of Faith and her kitten.

The firemen advised him that nothing could have survived the bomb damage, but Father Ross headed for where he estimated the basement would be, calling Faith's name. There was a faint answering miaow. Although the smouldering roof was threatening to collapse on him at any second, he began to pull aside fallen timbers. Moments later, he discovered Faith surrounded by smoking rubble, happily nursing her kitten. Neither was harmed in any way. Father Ross carried them to safety in the undamaged tower. As he was doing so, the church roof finally collapsed, reburying the area of the basement where the cats had been sheltering.

Father Ross commemorated this extraordinary series of events with a specially commissioned framed photograph of Faith prominently displayed when the church opened for business again. He captioned it with the words:

'Faith'

Our dear little church cat of St Augustine and St Faith. The <u>bravest</u> cat in the world.

On Monday, 9 September 1940, she endured horrors and perils beyond the power of words to tell.

Shielding her kitten in a sort of recess in the house (a spot she selected three days before the tragedy occurred), she sat the whole frightful night of bombing and fire, guarding her little kitten.

The roofs and masonry exploded. The whole house blazed. Four floors fell through in front of her. Fire and water and ruin all round her.

Yet she stayed calm and steadfast and waited for help. We rescued her in the early morning while the place was still burning, and by the mercy of Almighty God, she and her kitten were not only saved, but unhurt.

God be praised and thanked for His goodness and mercy to our dear little pet.

So, what just happened here? The clue is that phrase in Father Ross's tribute: *selected three days before*. The London Blitz was not something everybody had been expecting. If anything, it came about largely by accident. What everyone *had* been expecting was a German invasion of Britain. For this, Hitler needed control of the air and instituted a policy of bombing British airfields, in an attempt to cripple the RAF. On one raid in late August, Nazi planes wandered off course and bombed some London houses by mistake. The following night, Churchill ordered a retaliatory raid on Berlin.

Hitler lost his temper and demanded the Luftwaffe begin an immediate civilian blitz on London. The first anybody in Britain knew about it was when the bombs started falling on 7 September.

But Faith knew about it three days before. What was more, she knew the church was going to be hit and the basement would be the only safe place to take shelter. I might even reasonably speculate that she knew the priest would rescue Panda and herself from the rubble: after all, Father Ross remarked how calm she seemed with smoke and flames all around her.

The question is, how did she know?

We've already seen that cats may be telepathic, but telepathy is not the answer here. Father Ross did not know the Blitz was coming. London itself did not know the Blitz was coming. But Faith knew it was coming.

There is only one logical answer. Faith was a precognitive cat. She could see into the future.

But, logical or not, it is an answer that leads us into dangerous uncharted territory. For if cats demonstrate abilities like telepathy and precognition, who knows of what else they may show themselves capable?

Goosed by a Ghost

You know how it is. You're sitting with your cat on a dark and stormy winter's night, reading *Dracula* or *Salem's Lot*, when the mog suddenly sits up and takes notice. But of what? She is staring intently into an empty corner.* 'What?' you demand. 'What are you looking at?' But since you're no Pea Horsley, your cat does not respond. Instead, she follows with her eyes as something (some Thing) emerges invisibly from the corner and moves inexorably in your direction . . .

Incidents like this have been reported in their thousands by cat-owners across the globe, leading to the widespread belief that cats are endowed with what my Scots friends call the Sight, or Second Sight – the ability to see spirits, fairies, demons and other creatures of the night. But can they really? There is a case study from my personal files, previously

* There is an excellent example of this behaviour on YouTube at https://www.youtube.com/watch?v=tMahrwZDDZo

unpublished, that gives me reason to believe they might . . .

It was a nervous little group. None of the members had ever been to a séance before, except the organisers – and their experience was limited. They were a young British couple, Harriet and Roderick, in the second year of their marriage, with a recently discovered interest in spiritualism.

Each approached the subject from a different direction. Roderick worked as a journalist and was currently building a reputation as an investigative reporter. His instincts told him there might be a story in spiritualist claims to contact the dead. Harriet's interest was more personal. Prior to their marriage, she had worked for a mortgage broker and rented rooms in a large Georgian terrace house within easy reach of her office. Her live-in landlady, Irene, was a spiritualist medium. She once commented on Harriet's 'psychic abilities', which she felt Harriet should develop by taking mediumistic training. Harriet was intrigued, but a little frightened.

Harriet never did take formal training, but after their marriage Roderick encouraged her interest in psychism and they attended a few professional séances together, all of which proved something of a disappointment.

'The trouble is, you can never be sure they aren't faking it,' said Roderick, when they discussed their experience afterwards. 'Even if you never managed to expose them, that could only mean you never found the trick.'

'Unless you held the séance yourself,' Harriet suggested. 'Then you could make sure there was no fakery involved.'

Roderick took fire on the idea and tried to persuade Harriet to act as the medium. When she flatly refused, they fell to discussing alternatives. One thought was to hold a séance without a medium.

The classic spiritualist séance consists of a medium and several sitters ranged around a table in a poorly lit or completely darkened room. Typically, the medium will fall into a trance to make contact with the spirit world, then pass on messages from the dead to one or more of the sitters. Sometimes the process will be accompanied by what spiritualists call 'phenomena' – knocks on the table, inexplicable breezes, weird lights and so on. Occasionally, small objects or the table itself might be persuaded to move of their own accord, or even levitate. All of this is attributed by spiritualists to the power of the spirits, channelled through the person of the medium. Was any of it possible without one?

In the hope of finding an answer, Roderick investigated devices like the Ouija board and the planchette, both of which promised spirit contact without the need to call on the services of a medium. A Ouija board – the name is a combination of French and German meaning 'Yes, yes' – features the letters of the alphabet, the numbers 0 to 9 and the words *yes* and *no*. It is used with a heart-shaped pointer, mounted on rollers so that it can move easily in any direction. When working alone, you place one hand lightly on the pointer, try to relax and allow the pointer to move, apparently of its own accord, to spell out messages from the beyond. A planchette looks something like the Ouija pointer, but without the board and with a pencil, ball-point, or other writing implement attached to the tip. Set the device on a sheet of paper, rest one hand lightly on it and relax. Given luck and patience, it too will move to produce spirit messages, written on the paper.

Although both devices avoided the need for a medium, neither was perhaps ideal. Roderick's journalistic cynicism persuaded him that, while there could be no conscious fakery with something you were using yourself, the possibility of self-deception loomed large. Any supposed spirit messages could originate in your unconscious mind so that you would essentially be talking to yourself.

But then Roderick discovered a variation on Ouija that seemed to offer a solution – glass moving. In this form of séance, a glass tumbler is placed upside down on a polished table, ringed by the alphabet on printed cards. (He used a Lexicon deck, but handwritten letters on scraps of paper would have done just as well.) Each sitter is invited to rest the tip of a forefinger lightly on the base rim of the glass. After a time, the glass would begin to move and finally track to the letters to spell out messages.

Although the approach might seem a little home-made when compared with something as sophisticated as a planchette, it had some important advantages. First, it was designed to work with a small group, which left the door open for peripheral séance-room phenomena, like raps and breezes, which usually only occur in a group environment. Second, it allowed easy checking for potential fraud: anyone suspected of pushing the glass could be exposed immediately by asking them to remove their finger. Perhaps most importantly, self-deception could automatically be ruled out. Roderick checked with a professional psychiatrist about that one. The psychiatrist said he did not think it possible for an individual sitter to influence the glass unconsciously since he would be battling against the unconscious minds of all the other sitters with their own ideas about where the glass should go. Finally, while a glass-moving group could certainly involve a medium, all Roderick's investigations showed it did not actually need one.

He talked things over with Harriet and they decided to go ahead. Since only a limited number of fingers will fit comfortably on the base of a glass, they settled on an experimental group of six – themselves and four trust-worthy friends with an interest in the subject matter. When they got down to details, the friends chosen were two couples of an age similar to their own, providing a balance of the sexes that seemed somehow appropriate.

On the evening of the séance, Roderick set up the glass and cards on a polished dining table and explained to their friends exactly what was planned. As he was doing so, the group was joined by a seventh member, Roderick and Harriet's cat, Ned.

Ned was a four-year-old neutered tom who had belonged to Harriet before the marriage, a sociable, tiger-striped mog of indeterminate pedigree. He sniffed a greeting to each of their guests in turn, then jumped up on the back of an armchair and fell asleep.

Roderick dimmed the lights and the three couples took their places around the table. After some preliminary chat on what was about to happen, each sitter placed the tip of his or her forefinger on the bottom rim of the glass and waited.

And waited.

'Is anybody there?' asked Roderick, aloud, feeling a little foolish.

And waited.

After twenty minutes, the little group was showing clear signs of impatience. 'How long before someone makes contact?' asked a sitter named Brian.

'No idea,' admitted Roderick. 'I think it varies.'

'How long are we prepared to wait?' asked Brian's wife, Celia.

Roderick didn't know the answer to that either, but fortunately the glass took that opportunity to move. It wasn't much of a movement, something akin to a slight shudder, but it was enough to bring a ray of hope. A moment or two later, it made a small slide across the table, followed by a much more vigorous movement as far as one of the alphabet cards. 'You're pushing it!' exclaimed Joanna, another of the sitters, looking at her husband, George.

'No, I'm not,' George protested, frowning.

Roderick believed him. The glass had begun to circle the letters with such forceful speed that the sitters were having difficulty keeping contact. After several circuits, it slowed to pause briefly at each card, as if inspecting the letter on it. When it had finished, it returned to the centre and sat still.

'Is someone there?' asked Roderick, more confidently this time.

The glass moved swiftly to spell out N . . . O. 'At least it's got a sense of humour,' George remarked.

Things settled down after that. Roderick repeated the 'anybody there' question and this time got a sensible answer. When he asked who, the glass spelled out, 'The Gatekeeper'. It sounded like something out of fantasy fiction until Harriet explained spiritualists believed there was a class of spirit that acted as a sort of guardian of mediums, controlling access by those trying to make contact, so that the medium would not be overwhelmed. Such controls were often called 'gatekeepers'.

'Is one of us acting as a medium?' Roderick asked quickly.

'Y-E-S.'

'Who?'

'H-A-R-R-I-E-T.'

Roderick gave his wife a knowing look.

It proved slow going waiting for answers to be spelled out letter by letter, but three-quarters of an hour later a picture was beginning to emerge. The only post-mortem communication purported to originate from George's long-dead uncle, who delivered a trite description of life in Summerland, believed by spiritualists to be the after-death state. Roderick found it unimpressive, but George seemed happy to have been singled out for a message of any sort. Far more interesting, however, was what came through for Harriet. The Gatekeeper told her she did indeed have psychic talents, and to help her develop them, those on the 'other side' had appointed a guide, who was even now waiting in the wings, eager to communicate. After Harriet gave the go-ahead, the glass began to spell out messages from a spirit who introduced herself as Carmen, an eighteenth-century Spanish nun. The next half-hour or so was taken up with questions designed to elicit more information about Carmen and her new relationship with Harriet.

It was all very fascinating and not a little spooky, but some of the sitters were wary of the information – notably Roderick and Joanna, George's wife. Although he did not express his misgivings aloud, it occurred to Roderick that little being told to Harriet could be subject to historical investigation. Carmen was evasive when it came to details of her life. Joanna's suspicions showed through the questions she asked. 'Are you a spirit?'

'Y-E-S.'

'Are you making the glass move or are we?'

'I D-I-R-E-C-T T-H-E G-L-A-S-S B-U-T I-T I-S Y-O-U-R P-O-W-E-R T-H-A-T M-O-V-E-S I-T.'

'Can you prove you are who you say you are?'

'H-O-W?'

'Are you present in spirit form in this room?'

'Y-E-S.'

'Can you attract Ned's attention?'

At once Ned awoke, jumped down from the back of his chair and raced three times around the room, fur standing up in panic, before disappearing through a part-open window into the night. The sitters were so upset by this spectacular confirmation of a spirit presence that they closed down the séance forthwith. Ned returned some hours later, none the worse for being goosed by a ghost, but wary of the room where the séance had been held.

The story was not the only case study that persuaded me to take seriously the curious connection between cats and spirit presences. Another involved a personal experience with no apparent linkage to cats but which eventually opened up a whole field of speculation about the extent of feline perceptions and perhaps offered more clues to the popularity of the cats themselves.

The Kitten and the Phantom

Scientific research has shown conclusively that feline perception of the world differs considerably from that of humans. This difference may include detecting things we don't even suspect may be there.

Take night vision, for example. Cats don't just see a little better in the dark than we do: they can see *seven times* better than we can. Their evolutionary path has equipped them with something called a *tapetum lucidum,* an optical layer that reflects light back into the retina, effectively optimising every last photon. Furthermore, since the publication of a 2014 study, scientists have come to realise a significant number of those photons are floating in the ultraviolet end of the spectrum, which means cats can see a whole world that is quite invisible to us.

And it doesn't end there. Cats have thirty-two muscles in their ears. You have six and they don't work very well. A cat can swivel its ears independently backwards, forwards and sideways to focus on the slightest sound. From this you could likely deduce a cat can hear better than you, but you might be surprised to discover how much better. At the lower end of the scale, you're both much of a muchness, so you and your cat will hear a bass or baritone equally well. But when it comes to the higher register, he has you beaten hollow. Your cat can register sounds up to 64 kHz, some 1.6 octaves higher than anything you can manage and a full octave higher than a dog. So your cat not only sees a higher spectrum world than yours, but listens in to it as well.

And it doesn't end there. Cats have twice as many receptors in the cells of their noses as you do, plus the extra scent organ built into the roofs of their mouths. Put together, these two factors ensure your cat's sense of smell is fourteen times stronger than yours. So if a ghost exists on a higher vibration, as we are often told by spiritualists and other investigators of the paranormal, your cat will see it coming, hear it coming and probably smell it coming as well. When it gets close, I'm betting your cat can feel it too. Those whiskers will detect the slightest movement of the air to a degree at which a cat can literally feel an object without actually touching it.

Of course, all this simply suggests that cats may be well equipped to sense spirits. It doesn't prove that they actually do. (Ned's reaction may have been a coincidence.) But several years ago I stumbled on a report of a really odd scientific study with interesting implications for the whole troubled question. What led me to the study was really odd as well. When I was twenty-two years old, I had an out-of-body experience.

I awoke in the small hours of the morning with a need to urinate. I climbed out of bed, taking care not to waken my wife, and headed for the bathroom, only to find I could not open the bedroom door. For a moment I thought it was locked, but dismissed the idea since neither my wife nor I ever locked the bedroom. All the same, try as I might, the door remained stubbornly closed. I decided there must be something wrong with the closure mechanism and bent to take a closer look. At this point I discovered *my hand had penetrated the door knob*. The knob looked solid, but my fingers were sinking into it as if it was a hologram.

The bedroom was well lit by moonlight streaming through a gap in the curtains and as I looked around me in bewilderment, I noticed something else strange: there was a man lying in bed beside my wife.

You may recall the moment you heard your recorded voice played back for the first time and did not recognise it as your own. This was one such moment. I was outraged until I realised the man looked vaguely familiar. Even so it took another moment before the truth dawned: I was looking at myself. Or, to be more precise, I was looking at my physical body, fast asleep in the bed.

I have told this story many times since it happened, but seldom without being interrupted at this point by questions about my reactions. Weren't you frightened? Weren't you confused? Weren't you bewildered? The fact is I might well have been, were it not for one over-riding consideration – my need of a pee was growing more urgent with every passing minute. What actually occurred to me was that it would not be possible for me to pee in the bathroom if I left the relevant equipment behind. Clearly, I had to bring my body with me.

I returned to the bed and lay down, carefully realigning myself with my physical body. When I felt comfortably back to normal, I climbed out of bed again and hurried to the bathroom. Everything seemed as it should be. I could even feel the bedroom carpet underneath my feet. But this time when I reached the door, I passed right through it.

I turned on my (phantom) heel and re-entered the bedroom, again passing through the closed door. Sure enough, my physical body was still in the bed. Despite the pressure on my bladder, I took time to consider. The most important thing to report was that I felt completely solid, physical and real, normal in every respect. (Except, of course, for my new-found ability to pass through doors.) While I could *see* another body in my bed, I was not otherwise aware of it — it fed me no sensations. Nonetheless, logic dictated that I had left my physical body and was now functioning like a ghost. Oddly, it never occurred to me that I might have died. My bladder signals were far too urgent for that. I headed back to the bed, realigned myself very carefully indeed to make certain I was once again in my normal physical body. Then, with a huge feeling of relief, I made for the bathroom to empty my bladder.

This time I passed through both bedroom and bathroom doors before it dawned on me that I had still left my physical body behind.

I'll not draw out this ridiculous story. My next try found me standing at the toilet bowl before I realised yet again I had not succeeded in rousing my physical self. It took yet another attempt before I finally brought the reluctant corpse with me.

I spent much of the following day trying to come to terms with what had happened to me. I quickly ruled out the possibility that I'd been dreaming. Although this is the glib explanation frequently put forward for almost any unusual experience, the reality is that most of us are perfectly capable of differentiating between sleep and waking states and I am no exception. But if I had not been dreaming, what had actually happened to me? Had I *really* left my physical body and wandered the world like a ghost? And had anybody else ever done the same thing? My attempts to answer these questions opened up a whole new world of investigation and, incidentally, led me to publish my first-ever book.

What happened to me used to be called *astral projection* and still is in esoteric circles. For most of those who use the term, what you see is what you get: you are equipped with a second subtle body, which can, in certain circumstances, detach from the physical and carry your consciousness wherever it chooses to wander. This astral body is a mirror image of the more familiar you, but mostly quite invisible to anyone you may happen to meet on your travels.

Occult students suspect it is the astral body that leaves the physical at the point of death, but that you don't have to die to detach. In 1886, a founder of the Society for Psychical Research, Frederic William Henry Myers, co-authored a two-volume work entitled *Phantasms of the Living*.* While his fellow authors plumped for telepathic hallucinations as an explanation of the reports they cited, Myers believed the phantasms had an objective existence and occupied regions of physical space . . . tantamount to claiming them as astral bodies.

Today, however, the term has fallen from favour among researchers, who have largely replaced it with *out-of-body experience* or *OOBE*. They believe this label is better because it is more neutral. To talk of an OOBE allows you to acknowledge that some people have the sensation of leaving their physical bodies without necessarily accepting the theory of an astral vehicle – or indeed any other preconceived explanation.

When I say *some* people have the sensation, I may be guilty of understatement by implication. A relatively recent (1984) postal survey, carried out by the psychologist Susan Blackmore, suggested as many as one in ten people will have an OOBE at some point in their lives.

---

* Frederic W. H. Myers, Frank Podmore and Edmund Gurney, *Phantasms of the Living*, Trübner, 1886.

Earlier polls have produced even more startling figures. A 1954 student survey showed 27.1 per cent of respondents had had an out-of-body experience, the majority of them more than once. Scientist Celia Green's study of Oxford undergraduates in 1968 showed an even higher (34 per cent) figure. Both surveys were conducted on a small, selective base, but in 1975 a far wider sampling was taken. This showed a 25 per cent rate of OOBE among students and a 14 per cent rate among the general population. Even these figures may be only the tip of an iceberg. When, in 1976, a mass-circulation North American publication appealed for information on the subject, 700 out of 1,500 replies claimed out-of-body experiences — a staggering 46.6 per cent.

OOBEs can happen to anybody; and have happened to Tolstoy, Churchill, the British intellectual and broadcaster Melvyn Bragg, and even the arch-sceptic James Randi. Randi found himself spread-eagled directly underneath the ceiling of his bedroom, looking down on his cat Alice, who was curled up on the cerise counterpane of his bed. His physical body lay beside her. Predictably, Randi dismissed the experience as a dream,* partly because he subsequently discovered his usual counterpane had been changed for one featuring a hunting scene – something he had inexplicably failed to notice when he went to bed – and partly because Alice had apparently been banned

* https://www.youtube.com/watch?v=1NwKkbd2e-c

from the house for the comfort of a guest who was allergic to cats.

But the problem with phantoms is that nobody can say with certainty exactly what they are: dreams, hallucinations (telepathic or otherwise), spirits of the dead, astral bodies of the living, or even what the Tibetans call *tulpa*s, fictional creations that somehow take on an independent life of their own.[*] Consequently, a good deal of scientific psychical research has been undertaken with the aim of finding out. Some of the most intriguing involved Dr Keith Harary.

In 1973, Harary, a trained psychologist and cat-lover, was involved in a series of experiments carried out by Dr Robert Morris under the auspices of the Psychical Research Foundation in North Carolina. Morris was interested in testing the most common OOBE theory of all – that your spirit/soul/astral body really does separate from the physical. Harary was an ideal test subject since he claimed to be able to induce an OOBE at will. What Morris then set out to do was attempt to detect the second body when Harary sent it to a prearranged target location.

Harary's pulse, blood pressure, galvanic skin response, breathing, eye movements and brain waves were all monitored during these attempts. The target

---

[*] For a fuller discussion of this remarkable phenomenon, see J. H. Brennan, *Whisperers: the Secret History of the Spirit World*, Overlook, New York, and Duckworth, London, 2013.

room approximately half a mile away was packed with thermistors, photo multipliers and various devices for measuring electrical conductivity and magnetic permeability.

When Harary reported that he was out of the body, his heartbeat and respiration increased while his blood pressure dropped. There was a similar decrease in galvanic skin response. Some rapid eye movements were noted, but he was not asleep, since the EEG showed a steady alpha rhythm, associated with relaxed alertness.

Scientists monitoring the various detection instruments in the target lab subsequently reported that Harary had failed to influence any of them — except one. Alongside the mechanical devices was a caged kitten, Harary's own pet, appropriately named Spirit. Harary had been instructed to soothe it by stroking if he was successful in visiting the lab. Spirit mewed thirty-seven times during a control period, but not at all during the four minutes when Harary reported stroking it while he was out of the body.

Morris found the results sufficiently significant to repeat the experiments in 1978, adding a gerbil, a hamster and a snake to the experimental kitten. Here again, over a series of tests, the kitten calmed down when Harary reported he was stroking it.*

* The snake, by contrast, actually struck into mid-air in the place where Harary reported his non-physical body was located.

The Morris experiments are often quoted as evidence for the detectable reality of a subtle 'astral body', capable of existing, like a ghost or a spirit, outside the physical. Less often mentioned is a logical corollary: if a kitten's reactions can be used to detect a phantom, it must mean the kitten can see (or sense) the phantom in the first place.

In other words, whatever else they may tell us about OOBEs, the Morris experiments provide evidence for another psychic power to emerge from the mysterious world of cats. Nor does sensing phantoms complete the list.

Hypnotic Cat

Except for staring at spirits, cats tend to be secretive about their paranormal abilities. I very much doubt that Faith would ever have revealed her precognitive powers had she not found herself facing a life-threatening emergency and a stubborn owner who insisted on repeatedly carrying her kitten back into danger. But no secret has ever been so well preserved as the cat's ability to hypnotise, when such a talent may surely provide some explanation of the feline's fascination for humanity.

Although Irish author Tony Locke assures us[*] that 'Some people believed that the cat had supernatural powers and could hypnotise you', a trawl of your Google results will quickly produce categorical denials. The suggestion that a cat might fascinate a bird, for example, is dismissed as an old wives' tale or at best an outmoded belief. But if you persevere you will eventually stumble on clues to the truth. Like the entry in the SuperHeroHype

[*] In Tony Locke, *Irish Ghost Tales*, The History Press, 2015.

forum from a cat-owner who claims to have witnessed cat hypnosis in action.[*]

As he tells it, he went out to look for his cat in the yard and came upon him staring at a bird in a tree. As he watched, the bird became hypnotised and fell off its branch; it lay on the ground until the cat dragged it 'very lovingly and tenderly' into the shade of another tree. Then it ate it.

In 1894, Dr James R. Cocke published his master-work, *Hypnotism: How It Is Done; Its Uses and Dangers*, and opened a chapter on 'Hypnotism in the Lower Animals' with the blunt statement that certain animals have the power to fascinate their prey; and by 'fascinate' he makes clear that he means hypnotise. Most animals, he claims, are capable of being hypnotised, but he mentions only two (apart from humans) that have the ability to induce the hypnotic state. One is the snake, which isn't very good at it.[†] The other is our old friend the cat.

The good doctor was sufficiently intrigued to embark on a series of experiments in which one of his students studied the behavioural characteristics of a hypnotising feline and concluded that 'The eye of a cat occupies the same relation to a bird that a bright coin does to a man. The cat's pupils become dilated in watching a bird and the bird, although flying in circles during most of the

[*] http://forums.superherohype.com/showthread.php?t=227952
[†] In an experiment, the reptile managed to influence only six out of 100 frogs.

time, keeps its eyes fixed as far as possible upon those of the cat.'

Dr Cocke goes on to report:

Some years ago I purchased a stuffed cat. A student hid it in some bushes on a farm so that the head, eyes and forepaws were mainly visible, while the rest of the body was concealed. A bird sitting on a tree, as soon as it perceived the stuffed cat, first appeared to be frightened, then began flying in circles round the cat, each successive circle smaller than the last.

Finally the bird lit upon the ground within fourteen inches of the cat's face, and looked steadily into its glass eyes. Its attention was fixed, its pupils somewhat dilated, and so absorbed was it that it did not fly until the student, stepping carefully, passed between it and the cat. This experiment was repeated on nine different occasions with different birds and the same phenomenon was obtained eight times.

Although it's disturbing to discover you could perhaps be hypnotised by a dead cat, one might reasonably ask how important this is in the grander scheme of things. Even if every (living) cat on the planet turns out to be a skilled hypnotist, they can't actually make you do anything you wouldn't do in the waking state. Can they?

A consensus of internet sites claiming expertise in the subject says you can't be made to do anything under hypnosis that runs contrary to your moral principles. This is an idea rooted in a nineteenth-century demonstration by the great French neurologist Jean-Martin Charcot. While teaching a class of medical students at the University of Paris, Charcot hypnotised a pretty servant girl. In the middle of the demonstration, he was called away and left the class in the charge of one of the students. This young man failed to display the integrity and maturity for which medical students are so widely noted and promptly ordered the hypnotised girl to take all her clothes off. The girl woke from her trance at once and slapped his face.

But while it's comforting to believe you can't be persuaded into something that goes against the moral grain, it's also nonsense. Charcot's student just didn't know how to do it properly. During the 1950s, a respectable Swedish businessman was kidnapped and subjected to repeated hypnosis, suggesting he robbed a bank. His kidnappers broke his will so effectively over the course of several weeks that he not only robbed the bank, but also shot the cashier. *

Ten years later, a group of London-based psychologists conducted a series of experiments to find out if it would be possible to use hypnosis to persuade a volunteer housewife to throw what she was told was acid into the face of a laboratory assistant. They managed to do

---

* Herbie Brennan, *Strange Powers of the Human Mind*, Faber & Faber, 2006.

so by convincing her, in her trance, that the man was about to murder her child.[*]

(For your peace of mind, I suppose I should explain that the beaker the woman was given contained a harmless liquid, substituted for the acid she was shown earlier. For the sake of completeness, I suppose I should also mention that on one run of the experiment the psychologists neglected to exchange beakers and the lab assistant had to be treated for burns.)

Of course, the average cat would have a hard time kidnapping a human victim or, for that matter, communicating the sort of complex suggestions needed to produce the desired effect. Except for one thing. We've already noted some cats at least seem to be adept at telepathy; and there is considerable evidence to suggest that telepathic hypnosis is a possibility.

The earliest recorded example dates back to the Marquis de Puységur, an eighteenth-century French nobleman and follower of Franz Anton Mesmer, a Viennese doctor who believed he could effect cures by means of an invisible magnetic fluid. The marquis was attempting to apply Mesmer's methods when he accidentally hypnotised a shepherd boy while trying to magnetise him. In subsequent experiments, the marquis discovered that his entranced subjects were sometimes as susceptible to suggestions uttered mentally as those spoken aloud.

[*] *Ibid.*

One subject in particular, a girl named Madeline, was particularly sensitive and could be made to walk, sit or pick up a specific object, all on purely mental commands. De Puységur was even able to pass control of Madeline to others. Once he did so, she obeyed their mental commands as well.

De Puységur took the precaution of tying his shepherd boy to a tree before beginning the hypnotic induction, something obviously beyond the capabilities of the average cat. But if it's possible to *command* hypnotised subjects by telepathy, might it also be possible to *hypnotise* them by telepathy in the first place?

That was precisely the thought that occurred to six well-fed (but apparently sober) academics at a dinner party in 1886. Among those around the table were Professor Pierre Janet, a prominent French psychologist who advocated the use of hypnosis for mental disorders, Frederic Myers, who founded the British Society for Psychical Research and is the man credited with inventing the word 'telepathy', the psychologist Julian Ochorowicz and a Le Havre doctor named J. H. A. Gilbert. All four were noted for their interest in the paranormal.

At the time, Dr Gilbert had been involved in a series of experiments with a peasant woman named Léonie, who, he discovered, could be hypnotised simply by pressing her hand . . . but only if Gilbert concentrated. This led to the idea that it wasn't so much the hand pressure that counted, but some sort of 'thought pressure'

Gilbert generated. He put it to the test and found he could hypnotise Léonie by thought alone – no physical contact was necessary.

Intrigued by Dr Gilbert's story, the men at the dinner party began to discuss whether it might be possible for the doctor to hypnotise Léonie by telepathy there and then, even though she wasn't in the house where they were dining. Gilbert agreed to try and went off to his study to concentrate. The remaining five academics hurried off to surround Léonie's home, which was almost a mile away.

What happened next was both farcical and frightening.

As the five men skulked in the shadows, Léonie suddenly emerged from her house with her eyes tight shut and walked briskly to her garden gate. Then, for no apparent reason, she stopped, turned and walked back in again. The men subsequently discovered that just at that point Dr Gilbert allowed his concentration to waver and dozed off. (Ochorowicz remarked unkindly that this was due to the unaccustomed strain of thinking.)

The men waited, but after a few minutes when nothing happened they had a whispered consultation and Janet was elected to find out what was going on. He walked cautiously up the path to the house, but as he reached the front door it was flung open and he was almost knocked down by Léonie as she came out, walking very quickly. (Dr Gilbert had woken up again.)

The five scholars regrouped and set off in hot pursuit. Although her eyes were again shut, she somehow managed to avoid lampposts and negotiate traffic for fully ten minutes as she headed in the general direction of Dr Gilbert's home. But then she stopped dead and looked around with every sign of confusion. (Dr Gilbert had decided the experiment was a failure and started a game of billiards to amuse himself.)

The watchers decided not to interfere, and after a short time, Léonie fell into a trance again and continued on her hurried journey. (Dr Gilbert had resolved to give the experiment another try, abandoned his billiards and begun to concentrate again.)

The conclusion of the experiment was equally bizarre. With renewed confidence that something was happening, Gilbert went to his front door to see if Léonie was coming. As he opened it, she walked into him with such force that she knocked him to the ground. With her eyes still shut, she actually walked over him and ran through the house, shouting, 'Where is he? Where is he?'

Dr Gilbert picked himself up and called to her mentally. Léonie heard and answered him.[*]

This spectacular example of telepathic hypnosis is not the only one on record. Intrigued by what he'd seen, Professor Janet experimented with Léonie and found that he, too, could place her in a trance from the other

[*] *Ibið.*

side of Le Havre just by thinking of her. And, like Gilbert, he could call her to him. Nearly a century later, during the Cold War, Russian scientists experimented successfully with telepathic hypnosis in the hope of influencing American politicians at a distance. Dr Edward Naumov, a Soviet parapsychologist, recorded an experiment in which a volunteer was successfully commanded to fall ten times out of ten using telepathy. Eight times out of the ten he fell in the specific direction commanded.[*]

If humans can do it – and clearly they can – you may be quite sure there is a cat somewhere that can do it too. But while the concept of strange feline powers is fascinating to contemplate, and vital to our investigation, even telepathic hypnosis fails to explain why humanity as a whole has become enthralled with *Felis catus*.

And enthralled we are, for we treat cats in a way we would never dream of treating any other animal — as we shall see in our next chapter.

[*] *Ibid.*

Servants and Masters

A series of events that began in early 2007 resulted in the placement of a cat in a senior executive position within the national transport network of a major industrialised country. What are we to make of the human impulse that allowed – indeed facilitated and encouraged – those events to happen?

The country was Japan. The network infiltrator was a cat called Tama.

The official story is that Tama was born in Kinokawa, Wakayama Prefecture, in 1999. The reality is that she appeared as part of a group of strays living near the small, poorly financed Kishi railway station. For five years she fed on scraps provided by rail passengers before she managed to seduce Toshiko Koyama, the acting station master. After she moved in, her prospects suffered a setback when it was announced that the station might have to close due to its financial problems.

In the event, closure was avoided due to pressure of public opinion, but just two years later the station was partially de-staffed as part of wide-ranging cost-cutting measures. Less than a year after that, with the railway seeking to cut costs even further, local admirers began lobbying to have Tama appointed as Kishi's station master. They pointed out that the only capital outlay would be the cost of a new station master's hat, while the only ongoing expense was cat food. It says much for their persuasive powers – and the popularity of cats in Japan – that railway management accepted these arguments and officially named Tama station master on 5 January 2007. Her main duties were listed as wearing the hat and greeting passengers.

At this point, the cat-lovers – and perhaps the cat – had achieved their original objective. A cat had been successfully placed in an executive position in a major transport network. Not only had anyone failed to object, but growing numbers of the general public were actively supporting the venture. One reason was that people had quickly become aware of what a fine job Tama was doing in her new post. Passenger numbers were up 10 per cent, while the media coverage of her appointment had resulted in a billion-yen boost to the local economy. Clearly, this was a cat that deserved to go places.

Exactly one year after her initial appointment, Tama was promoted and moved into her own office, specially adapted to feline needs. The local mayor and the railway-company president both turned up at a ceremony to mark the event.

Only two years later, in January 2010, Tama was promoted again, this time to the post of operating officer.

She was now not just the only female to hold a managerial position in the Wakayama Electric Railway Company, but the first cat anywhere in the world to become a management executive of a railway corporation.

Tama died in June 2015, aged sixteen years. She was honoured with a Shinto funeral, given the posthumous title of Honourable Eternal Station Master, and awarded a third promotion – to the rank of a Shinto goddess. The station building at Kishi has been remodelled to resemble a cat's face. The post of Kishi station master has been inherited, without opposition or objection, by another cat.

But these were not the only recent examples of humanity's extraordinary behaviour towards cats.

A lazy, calculating cat. What is she thinking?

The acquisition of power in our Western culture almost always means exposing yourself to an established political process. In brief, this involves smiling a lot, making promises with your fingers crossed and telling people what they most want to hear, whether it's true or not. If this gets you elected, you can do more or less what you want for at least four years. As you may have realised, cats are temperamentally well suited to doing what they want, so it may come as no great surprise to learn that one has already achieved the post of joint leader of a major UK political party.

The party in question was founded in 1983 by David, Screaming Lord Sutch, and his election agent Tarquin Fin-tim-lin-bin-whin-bim-lim-bus-stop-F'tang-F'tang-Olé-Biscuitbarrel to fight the Bermondsey (south London) by-election. They came sixth with 97 votes, a result that might have had something to do with their choice of political name – the Official Monster Raving Loony Party.

Peculiar name or not, the OMRLP won its first seat (on Ashburton town council in Devon) when its candidate, Alan Howling Laud Hope, was returned unopposed. That was in 1987. In May 1991, the party successfully fought for Conservative seats on the East Devon district council and Sidmouth town council. On the by-election scene, the OMRLP began to show itself capable of polling substantial votes. Although not necessarily enough to win them seats,* this did attract media

---

* Or even save their deposits.

attention and helped establish them as a bona fide political party, albeit one often dedicated to lampooning the political process.

Those with knowledge and understanding of feline history will appreciate why cat-lovers must, at this stage, have begun to take notice of the OMRLP as a possible target for infiltration. The party had high-profile national recognition, and even a degree of sympathy among disillusioned voters. Its main policies – the abolition of income tax and the creation of a mobile parliament, which would travel throughout the country rather than remaining permanently in London – were ideals cats could support since they didn't care one way or the other. Most important of all, the party was sufficiently eccentric to make some relationship with cats a real possibility.

Their opportunity arose in 1999 with the regrettable death of Screaming Lord Sutch.

The party chairman and deputy leader at the time was Howling Laud Hope, who was one of only two nominees in the subsequent leadership election. The other was Hope's cat, a handsome ginger-and-white four-year-old tom named Catmando. After a brief election campaign, a poll was taken and the result was a tie with each candidate receiving 125 votes. As party chairman, Hope had the right to cast a deciding ballot, but instead of claiming the election for himself, he decided to share the leadership with Catmando.

Once elected, Catmando, like Tama, worked extremely hard to strengthen his position and further

Heaven alone knows what political ambitions. Consequently, the OMRLP flourished as never before and actually fielded fifteen candidates in the UK's 2001 general election.

One can only speculate how far this may have gone. Catmando as a potential Member of Parliament? Catmando in the cabinet? Catmando as prime minister? But, alas, Catmando met an untimely end as the result of a traffic accident during the summer of 2002. Since then, the OMRLP have campaigned for cat crossings on all major roads and proposed a law banning the use of 'Catmando' as a cat name 'because there can only be one'.

OMRLP party members took the election of Catmando in their stride, but a rather more controversial example of humanity's extraordinary relationship with cats has arisen in the wilds of Alaska, with the reported election of a moggy named Stubbs to the post of mayor in the sleepy little town of Talkeetna. The controversy arises out of the possibility that it may not be true.

The bare facts are these. On 15 July 2012, the respected news agency United Press International reported that a cat had been elected mayor of Talkeetna, Alaska, 'about fifteen years ago'. The story was taken up by various media worldwide, including NBC News.

On 11 September 2013, the *Alaska Dispatch News* claimed the reports were a scam, in an article that began 'Enough with the cat crap.'

Although the *Alaska Dispatch News* is a double Pulitzer Prize winner for its public-service reporting and, as the name implies, is actually published in Alaska, I choose to accept the account put forward by UPI and other distant sources for the following reasons:

- It makes a much more sensational and amusing story.
- It supports my thesis of a special relationship.
- It is the sort of thing that has happened elsewhere and may, despite everything, be true.
- Even if not, the fact that it has been taken seriously by large segments of the media is itself indicative of humanity's bizarre behaviour towards cats.

This account, stitched together from the original published sources and roundly ignoring the *Alaska Dispatch News*'s objections, is as follows.

In 1997, the manager of Nagley's General Store in the small town of Talkeetna, Alaska, was a cat-lover named Lauri Stec. One morning, as she reported for work, she found someone giving away kittens from a box in the parking lot. Lauri decided to have one and chose a cute little ginger tom with no tail. She christened him 'Stubbs' and took him home.

When Stubbs was three months old, Talkeetna was in the throes of a mayoral election. The nominated (human) candidates all proved so unpopular that a spontaneous campaign erupted, calling for Stubbs to be elected. On 18 July, he became mayor as the result of a postal vote.

Stubbs's contribution to feline politics has so far been passive. His strategy seems largely aimed at increasing his own popularity by attracting tourists, declining to raise taxes or otherwise interfere with Talkeetna's nine hundred inhabitants. He maintains his image as a cat of the people by taking a little drink – water laced with catnip, served in a wine glass – every afternoon in a local bar.

Stubbs is still alive – and still mayor – at the time of writing, having survived an assassination attempt by a dog that left him with a punctured lung and fractured sternum. It is a mark of his political popularity that his vet bills were met by a crowd-sourcing fund set up on the internet.

Whatever the ultimate truth of Stubbs's mayoral office, there is no doubt at all about human interest in infiltrating cats into mayoral posts. One charismatic Canadian cat, aptly named Tuxedo Stan, was actually backed by his own political party to further this end.

Stan was born in 2010 in Halifax, Nova Scotia, and immediately recruited a veterinarian, Dr Hugh Chisholm, to look after him. He was only two when his human admirers made it known that he was interested in running for mayoral office. As frequently happens with cats, Stan proved to have a human entourage dedicated to serving his every whim, and five of its members promptly formed the Tuxedo Party to back his bid for power.

Stan made international headlines when his followers announced his entrance into the mayoral race in the

Halifax election of 2012, establishing a powerful internet presence and attracting celebrity endorsements from personalities like Ellen DeGeneres. There were, of course, the usual humourless cat-loathers who were at pains to point out that Stan was an unregistered candidate, but this technicality did not prevent him garnering a massive support base in Halifax itself and across the internet.

Although he did not win the election, his influence was so profound that the city council subsequently voted in a $40,000 grant in his name to help establish a low-cost Halifax cat clinic.

Who knows how far Tuxedo Stan may have gone, but the strain of politics took a heavy toll. Less than a year after his failed election bid, he died from cancer. But his legacy lives on. The Tuxedo Party continues to flourish under the leadership of Stan's brother, the equally ambitious Earl Grey, whose supporters mounted a sophisticated, but ultimately unsuccessful, campaign for him to become Canada's prime minister in 2015.[*]

Another, arguably far more serious, pointer towards the unusual relationship between cats and people is the fact that so many of us have gone to a great deal of trouble to ensure our cats become rich. Take, for example, the case of Blackie, who shared a mansion

---

[*] https://www.youtube.com/watch?v=KUP3G-aEx1I

with fourteen other felines in the 1980s. Although the cats came and went as they pleased, the mansion was actually owned by a wealthy British antiques dealer named Ben Rea. One by one the cats died off until only Blackie remained, and when Rea died in 1988, Blackie found himself the beneficiary of a £7 million legacy, half of Rea's entire estate. The other half went to cat charities.[*]

Just eleven years after the Rea legacy, the marvellous British singer Dusty Springfield left a small fortune to her cat, Nicholas. I have been unable to discover exactly how much, but we all know that pop singers make millions (unlike authors) and the terms of her will – which included importing his favourite American baby food – would suggest substantial funds.[†]

The accumulation of feline wealth has continued into the twenty-first century. In the early years of the new millennium, a wealthy American widow named Margaret Layne fell under the spell of a stray tom cat called Tinker. So much so that she set up a $226,000 trust fund for his care and protection following her death in 2003. As if this wasn't enough, she left an additional endowment to her neighbours on condition that they use it to look after him. Tinker also inherited her house, valued at $800,000.[‡]

[*] http://www.catster.com/lifestyle/6-cats-inherit-fortunes-estate-planning-cat-care-facts
[†] *Ibid.*
[‡] *Ibid.*

In 2005, the United Church of Canada became the beneficiary of the $1.3 million estate of parishioner David Harper. They should have known there'd be a catch, for they also inherited Mr Harper's ginger tom, Red, with a bequest to cover his care, food and vet bills.*

The trend continues. In November 2013, an American television channel, WMC-TV, reported that two Tennessee cats, Frisco and Jake, had inherited the mansion they lived in from their newly deceased owner, Leon Sheppard Sr. He also left them a quarter of a million dollars to go towards its maintenance.[†]

When I first visited Rome, I was surprised not only by the large numbers of the city's street cats, but by how fit and well-fed they looked, reminiscent of Bob the street cat in the smash hit books and movie. Now, of course, I realise the richest cat in the world began his career as a Roman stray. Like so many before him, he made his fortune by ankle-polishing an unsuspecting human.

Tommaso the street cat experienced his change of circumstances when he met up with an elderly Italian heiress named Maria Assunta. Maria was widowed, childless and doubtless lonely when Tommaso turned on the charm. As a result, she took him in and devoted her declining years to his welfare. On her death in 2012, she left him her entire €13 million estate. But not

* *Ibid.*
† *Ibid.*

directly. Italian law forbids leaving that sort of money to an animal, so Maria made her will in favour of her nurse (a human being) on the understanding that it was really Tommaso's money. Tommaso now enjoys a life of luxury in a countryside property he shares with the nurse and a companion cat.*

To judge from the wealth of evidence presented, you have to wonder whether we keep cats at all. Maybe we're all living in a Matrix designed by cats to hide the fact they're keeping us.

* http://www.care2.com/greenliving/worlds-richest-cat.html

Cats Throughout History

As was ably demonstrated in the previous chapter, human reactions to cats can sometimes border on lunacy. Even at its best, we must admit the relationship between the two species has been marked by extremes and, to judge by the popularity of cats in cave paintings, endured for millennia – something that will merit closer examination later in this book. How on earth did such a situation come about? Perhaps we might find some clue from an examination of the relationship itself and how it has manifested throughout a long, sometimes troubled history.

Let us begin by setting our literary time machine to visit the Pliocene Epoch between 3.6 and 5.3 million years ago. Mammals had evolved by then, but there were few you would recognise on your morning walk, and even those that seemed familiar would mostly look extremely strange: giant camels, three-toed horses, enormous armoured mammalian glyptodons . . .

But if your walk took you into the rainforests of South East Asia, one creature would be instantly recognisable.

The basic design of the cat – supple, low-slung body, long tail, a hunter's teeth and claws – which appeared in the early Pliocene, proved so successful that it has remained more or less unchanged to the present day.

The nearest thing to a cat-owner in those distant times was a small, ape-like creature called an Australopithecine, now thought of as human, if only just. But the only evidence of a relationship with cats was that some of the larger ones liked to eat them.

This antagonistic situation held firm for several million years but possible evidence of a change eventually emerged in southern Cyprus where excavations of a 9,500-year-old burial have unearthed two skeletons: one of a human, the other of a cat. This is not, of course, conclusive proof that cats were domesticated 9,500 years ago – it's just possible some hardy Cypriot decided to reverse the natural order of things and eat a cat – but academics have their suspicions.

We know cats were domesticated eventually, but we don't know exactly where or when. Like so many other milestones on the road to civilisation, it may have happened in China. Fossil finds there, dating back 5,300 years, show there were cats similar in size to a twenty-first-century domestic feline, although whether they'd actually moved in with humans at this time is difficult to say.

We're on much firmer ground when we turn our attention to the Egyptians, whose meticulous record-keeping leaves us with little doubt that there was definitely a developed relationship between cats and humanity in the earliest days of their civilisation.

Ancient Egypt, according to the Greek historian Heroditus, was the 'gift of the Nile'. By this he meant that torrential annual rains in Ethiopia sent a deluge of floodwater northwards down the river to inundate vast tracts of land along its Egyptian banks. When the waters receded, they left behind deposits of thick black fertile mud so suited to the growing of grain that they turned Egypt into the breadbasket of the ancient world. Conventional wisdom holds that these facts have a bearing on the question of cat domestication.

Throughout the whole of its long history, Egypt was peppered with pharaonic grain stores, ready to distribute food to the populace as the need arose. In a well-ordered land, these were relatively easy to guard against human robbers, but impossible to protect against rodents. Until, that was, somebody noticed how efficient small wild cats were at killing rats and mice. (A modern study estimates the number of creatures – mice, birds, voles, chipmunks and so on – killed by domestic cats in America each year runs close to 25 *billion*.[*]) Academics speculate that this led to cats being encouraged to visit granaries, possibly even lured with scraps of food.

[*] http://www.huffingtonpost.com/2013/01/30/domestic-cats-kill-billions-mice-birds-annually-study_n_2575833.html

Was this the first step towards domestication? Did some soft-hearted grain guard bond with a visiting hunter, as the academics keep telling us? It sounds a reasonable explanation, and scholars have pushed it strongly. But could the protection of grain really explain what happened between our Egyptian ancestors and their cats?

For most of us, Egyptian religion is a blur of gods, mummies and tombs. Academics have worked hard to bring a little clarity to this impression and now claim they can distinguish four main lines of Egyptian religious thought.

The first and most obvious was the conviction that there was life after death, a belief that profoundly influenced the behaviour of Egyptians during their life before death, leading to the widespread practice of mummification and the construction of enormous, and enormously costly, tombs. The corpse had to be preserved because the souls – there were three of them, *ba, ka* and *ib* – couldn't really flourish without it. The tombs had to be enormous because they were where you lived after death and you wouldn't want to be stuck in cramped quarters for eternity, would you?

The religious practices that sprang out of the belief in life after death were complex, hallowed by tradition and sometimes really gross. Take mummification, for example, a process that was applied to cats as well as kings. This began with the embalmers splitting the dead feline's nose in order to insert a tube into the skull. The tube was then used to introduce solvents into the skull cavity. When the brain was part liquefied, they drew it out through the nostrils with an iron hook.

Whether you were human or cat, the job at this point involved removing your entrails. Cubit after cubit of glistening intestines were dropped into the nearest canoptic jar, the resulting cavity flushed out with palm wine and scented aloes stuffed up your bottom. The corpse then spent the next seventy days soaking in natron, a mineral salt much prized by the Egyptians for its desiccating qualities. Finally, it was tightly bandaged to become the familiar mummy.

The next thread of religious thought comes as something of a surprise. Behind the forest of gods so frequently portrayed in hieroglyphic inscriptions lies a vague backwash of monotheism, an ill-defined and seldom expressed belief in a single supreme deity. Even the academics fight shy of emphasising this one since its only overt expression seems to have been a disaster.

Somewhere around 1348, the reigning pharaoh changed his name from Amenhotep (*Amun is Satisfied*) to Akhenaten (*Effective for Aten*), dumped millennia of tradition and declared a doctrine of one God only, to be worshipped in His visible manifestation as the disc of the sun.

Akhenaten's theology taught that the sun ultimately gave birth to, and now sustains, all life on Earth. The only difference from the modern viewpoint is that he considered the sun to be a sentient entity and even that is held to be at least a possibility within the laws of quantum physics.

Egyptians were well used to doing what their pharaoh told them, so they went along with his nonsense as long as he was there to keep an eye on them. But that was only for about twelve years. After his death, the old order quickly returned to business as usual. The accession of his son to the throne was marked by another name change that said it all. Young Tutankhaten (*Living Image of Aten*) became Tutankhamun (*Living Image of Amun*). In little more than a decade, Akhenaten was being called 'the Enemy', his statues toppled and his name chiselled off monuments.

Some cats take themselves very seriously.

A third stream of religious thought holds that when the world was first created, part of the process was the establishment of *maat*. *Maat* is one of those irritating words that have no exact English equivalent. It sort of means divine order, but with overtones of harmony, stability, security, tradition, justice, truth and just plain rightness. Our modern idea of evolution – progress rooted in perpetual change – would have been a bewildering anathema to the Egyptians. To them, the natural order was changeless, a rightness established on the First Day that needed no adjustment.

Maat was sometimes challenged, of course. Day to day experience would teach you that. But you needn't worry, because any change must be temporary. *Maat* will always re-establish itself in the end.

The fourth stream was the conviction that Pharaoh wasn't just king, but god. Ancient Egypt, like pre-invasion Tibet, was a theocracy. But that didn't mean Pharaoh concerned himself with law-making for the good of his people on the basis of his infallibility. The people didn't need laws since everything was perfect (*maat*) already. The pharaoh's prime concern was to support the state of *maat* by means of time-honoured daily rituals held in temples throughout the land. Since even a god couldn't be everywhere at once, his priests deputised for him in most of them.

Put it all together and the academic picture presents you with an Egypt run by the Tory Party (in America read Republican) where the people had no say in anything and received as few benefits as possible. The reality was that while Pharaoh was leading his priests in maintaining the *maat*, the country was being run by a cat. Her name was Bast and she lived in Bubastis, a city called after her on the Nile delta.

Bast, or Bastet as she later became, was one of Ancient Egypt's oldest gods. Traces of her worship date back beyond 3000 BCE. She was the daughter of Ra and Isis, presiding primarily over cats and protection (notably of the home) but also ruling over family, joy, dance, music, sexuality, motherhood and fertility. Conventional wisdom has it that most, if not all, of these attributes arose out of the Egyptians' observation of cats' natural abilities. Preying on rodents as they did limited the spread of disease and they were capable of killing snakes, thus functioning as protectors of the family and the home. Anyone who has experienced the behaviour of a cat in heat will readily appreciate the association with sexuality. Anyone presented with a litter of five or six kittens will understand Bast's connection with fertility, while the exemplary behaviour of the mother cat in feeding and protecting those kittens must readily explain the linkage with motherhood in the minds of the Ancient Egyptians. (Strangely, the domestic cat's maternal instinct is shared by the tigress but not by the lioness, who will typically abandon her cubs for days on end, with a resultant high mortality rate.)

But there are more subtle associations not so easily explained. Bast's original manifestation was not that of a domestic cat, but of a lioness, suggesting hidden strengths behind the purring façade. The association with the occult and mysterious was there from earliest times. Numbered among Bast's four mythic siblings was Thoth, the ibis-headed god of moon and magic. Her son Khonsu was also a moon deity.

An even stronger association – one we shall be exploring more fully later in this book – was with the healing arts. Bast's written name contains the hieroglyph for ointment jar and she is frequently depicted carrying an *ankh*, the Egyptian symbol for life. An attribute of her brother Thoth is medical practice. Most intriguing of all is her son Nefertem, who manifests as a man (indicating Bast's close association with the human race) and is the primary Egyptian god of healing.

Like Pharaoh, Bast was a god (more precisely a goddess) incarnated in a living creature. Unlike Pharaoh, who was isolated from his subjects, apart from a few public appearances each year, Bast was the centre of attention each day. Every cat who died a natural death in Egypt was taken to Bubastis for mummification and burial. Pilgrims came in a steady stream to visit the shrine and make offerings to the smug little bundle of fur that was Bast's current representative on Earth. And festivals in honour of Bast were by far the most elaborate and costly ever held in the country. Heroditus described one in his *History of Egypt*:

Now, when they are coming to the city of Bubastis they do as follows: they sail men and women together, and a great multitude of each sex in every boat; and some of the women have rattles and rattle with them, while some of the men play the flute during the whole time of the voyage, and the rest, both women and men, sing and clap their hands; and when as they sail they come opposite to any city on the way they bring the boat to land, and some of the women continue to do as I have said, others cry aloud and jeer at the women in that city, some dance, and some stand up and pull up their garments.

This they do by every city along the river-bank; and when they come to Bubastis they hold a festival celebrating great sacrifices, and more wine of grapes is consumed upon that festival than during the whole of the rest of the year. To this place (so say the natives) they come together year by year even to the number of seventy myriads of men and women, besides children.

More wine . . . than the rest of the year is a major celebration by any measure, but even outside festivals, it's clear that *Felis catus* had engineered a very special relationship indeed with the Egyptian people. If your cat died a natural death, everyone in the household, men, women and children, was obliged to shave off their eyebrows as a sign of mourning. If you killed a cat, even accidentally, the penalty was death. Nor was this dead-letter legislation. The Greek historian Diodorus has left us an eyewitness account of a Roman soldier being executed for accidentally killing a cat, even though Pharaoh himself intervened on his behalf – an indication, I might point out in passing, of who was held in higher esteem, the cat or the King:

> The populace crowded to the house of the Roman who had committed the 'murder'; and neither the efforts of the magistrates sent by the King to protect him nor the universal fear inspired by the might of Rome could avail to save the man's life, though what he had done was admitted to be accidental. This is not an incident which I report from hearsay, but something I saw myself during my sojourn in Egypt.

The cat was considered so sacred that when a fire broke out, instead of running to douse it, Egyptians would typically form a phalanx to prevent any stray cat from stupidly wandering into the flames. Academics currently hold that the Ancient Egyptians considered *all* animals sacred; and certainly there were some – the crocodile and the ibis spring to mind – that had their own special cities and shrines. But none received anything like the respect and attention accorded to the cat.

So was this the beginning of the domesticated cat? We may never know for sure, but we do know that by about 2465 BCE a profound change occurred in the relationship between cats and men. That was the date Egyptians decided to declare the cat sacred. Henceforth, it became the focus of cults and was worshipped in the temples.

Some academics have pointed out that this does not necessarily mean cats were domesticated at this time, although they were obviously admired. The earliest known record to positively identify domestic cats dates to 1500 BCE, but thereafter there are plenty of indications that humanity's long journey with the cat had definitely begun. There are early (fifth and sixth century BCE) literary references to domestic cats in Greece and China and a few hundred years later they appear in the Sanskrit writings of India. By CE 600, there were domestic cats in Japan and across the Middle East. It took another few hundred years for *Felis catus* to reach Britain, but by CE 936 the Welsh prince Howel Dda was enacting legislation for their protection.

Which begs another form of our original question: why did cats become so important that they warranted the protection of a prince? Perhaps the answer lies somewhere in the overall history of human–cat relations . . .

The Spread of Cats

It lasted thousands of years, but all good things come to an end and the Egyptian civilisation was no exception. After only a few millennia of increasingly successful invasions by Nubians, Persians, Greeks and others, it became clear the writing was on the wall. Cats began to hunt for new servants to look after them ... and succeeded remarkably well in finding them.

In Ancient India, for example, they attempted to replicate the Egyptian experience by establishing the cat goddess Sastht, a protective deity and thinly disguised version of Bast, who quickly became almost as deeply revered. India's political structure did not permit the total takeover that happened in Egypt, but the high esteem in which the cat was held is reflected in the tradition that the god Indra himself once became a cat to escape from an angry husband. The story is told in the *Ramayana*, one of the two great literary epics of Ancient India, where the god Indra seduces the beautiful maiden Ahalya, then transforms himself into a cat as a means of avoiding the consequences. This is a very early example of a theme we shall return to later in this book – the shamanic implications of shape-shifting into the form of a cat. The legend also highlights the close relationship believed to exist between humans and cats in prehistoric India: a jealous husband would find nothing remarkable in discovering a pet cat in his wife's quarters. It's noteworthy, too, that our popular children's story 'Puss in Boots' ultimately derives from an Indian folk tale, originally told in the *Panchatantra*, another popular example of Indian literature dated sometime prior to the fifth century BCE. The original version clearly shows that the Ancient Indians looked on cats as both cunning and ruthless, yet in a strange way extremely useful to their human masters. The *Panchatantra* story also contains an element of shape-shifting, a curious talent that will appear mysteriously again and again in our investigations.

Cats managed to impress the Ancient Persians so successfully that for a time they actually believed the feline species had been created magically. The story went about that after the great Persian hero Rustam saved an elderly magician from a band of thieves, the old man asked what he would like as a thank-you gift. Rustam replied there was nothing he needed since he already had the comfort of his fire, the scent of the smoke and the beauty of the stars overhead. The magician then took a handful of smoke, added flame and brought down two of the brightest stars in the heavens, kneading them together and blowing on them. When he opened his hands, he was holding a small, smoke-grey kitten with eyes as bright as the stars and a tiny tongue that darted like the tip. of a flame. In this way, so the legend goes, the first Persian cat came to be created as a token of gratitude.

Cats generated an even more outrageous mythology after they managed to establish another Bast look-alike in China in the shape of the goddess Li Shou. Sacrifices were made to her for fertility and rodent control, and the legend grew that she embodied the importance of cats in the first days of the world. According to a Chinese creation story, in the beginning the gods made Heaven and Earth, then appointed cats to oversee them. At much the same time, they granted cats the power of speech.

Three times the gods came to check on how well the cats were getting on and each time found them asleep or at play. On the third visit, the cats explained they had better things to do than running the world and nominated human beings for the job. The power of speech was then taken from the cats and given to humans but, while they could talk nineteen to the dozen, humans seemed incapable of understanding a word the gods said to them. So cats remained entrusted with the task of maintaining order, which anyone could see made them vastly more important in the great scheme of things than silly old humans.

The legend is particularly interesting in that it encapsulates in a single rather charming story so many of the observable characteristics of domestic cats. Cats do indeed behave as if some deity had put them in charge of the world and they actually have a serious job to do in terms of rodent control. But instead of getting on with their work, house cats typically spend most of their time asleep or at play. If the whole of evolution can be summed up in the single question *when do we eat?*, domestic cats are clearly perfectly happy to pass on the problem of finding their food to their human contemporaries. Even when a human owner is tardy in this respect, the cat does not rush out to catch her own supper, but rather nags said owner into opening another pouch of cat food. Clearly she sees her role as one of keeping her owner in order. One might also speculate that humanity's initial lack of speech mentioned in the legend might echo to some extent our earlier discoveries about a telepathic aspect to feline–human communication.

In neighbouring Japan, meanwhile, it seemed as if cats achieved something close to the veneration they had received in Egypt – all due to their influence on one man. But that man was the Emperor, whose word was law, his prestige stratospheric.

A day came when a cat found himself in the Gotokuji temple in Tokyo's quiet Setagaya district as the royal entourage was approaching. When the Emperor came into view, the cat (presumably) sensed that a lightning strike was imminent.

The cat began to wave furiously to the Emperor, beckoning him to come into the safety of the temple.

Intrigued by such peculiar behaviour from an animal, the Emperor followed the cat inside . . . just in time to avoid the lethal bolt of lightning that struck the path he had been following. The grateful Emperor promptly proclaimed great honours for the cat, which henceforth earned his entire species a reputation for bringing good luck.

Japanese cats soon learned that being lucky was almost as good as being sacred. They came to be housed in private pagodas and were considered guardians of the home and protectors of books. Here again we have mysterious echoes of the mythic attributions given to cats in other apparently unrelated cultures: cats were venerated as guardians of the home in Ancient Egypt while the term 'protectors of books' may relate to our earlier speculation about communication. And it all got better and better as the years rolled on. Cats were eventually valued so highly that by the tenth century CE nobody but the mega-rich could afford to own one.

To this day, there is a flourishing *maneki neko* industry in Japan, dedicated to the manufacture and sale of cat dolls with one paw raised. Each *maneki neko*, which translates as 'the beckoning cat', represents the (cat) goddess of mercy and is firmly believed to attract good luck, particularly when given as a present. You see them prominently displayed in shops and restaurants all over Japan to attract customers.

They certainly attracted both good luck and custom-ers to the Gotokuji temple, which today displays about a thousand of them in various sizes and holds additional stocks for sale to tourists.

But back in the ancient Mediterranean, cats were beginning to lose ground as the remnants of Ptolemaic Egypt were absorbed into the Roman Empire. This was partly due to the Greek and Roman preference for weasels as a means of pest control. Although weasels are nowhere near as cute as cats, they *are* capable of being tamed and they *do* have strokable fur. Consequently, they provided at least a little competition for the felines.

The cats fought back, of course, and weaselled their way into many a Roman household where they quickly became popular pets. Sacrifices were made to cat gods at weddings and funerals, the former to ensure the happy couple a prosperous future and the latter to provide protection for the deceased in the afterlife. Romans greatly appreciated their cats' obvious independence: statues of Libertas, the goddess of liberty and freedom, often showed her with a cat at her feet. Cats were the only animals permitted entry into Roman temples but, try as they might, they never made it to sacred status. Eventually, with the barbarians massing at the city gates, it became clear Rome's days as a great power were numbered.

Some cats tried a rearguard action in Ancient Greece, where Bastet had been adopted from Ancient Egypt and added to the Greek pantheon under the name of Ailuros. The Greeks thought of Ailuros as a manifestation of their native deity Artemis, goddess of fertility and the hunt. One myth introduces the increasingly familiar theme of shape-shifting when Artemis transforms herself into a cat to escape a pursuing Titan. Interestingly, later myths show Artemis as a skilled practitioner of the magical arts, once again highlighting the mythic connection between cats and the occult. But worship of Ailuros never achieved anything like the popularity of Egypt's cult of Bast, and the reputation of cats in Greece nose-dived after Aristophanes started making fun of them in his plays.

Aristophanes, who was arguably the most popular Greek playwright of his day, clearly liked cats and often portrayed them in his plays as benign, friendly creatures. But he was first and foremost a satirist who found in felines a peg on which to hang parodies of his more pompous characters. He coined the expression 'the cat did it' as every villain's excuse for wrongdoing. It was a catchphrase that caught on widely and, as a result, the way cats were looked upon suffered. They saw the writing was on the wall and decided to ship out for greener pastures.

But where to go? One of the trickiest problems they had encountered in Ancient Greece (apart from Aristophanes, who blamed them for everything) was that the Greeks stubbornly associated them with death, darkness, evil and witches. When Greece became Christian, this was countered to some extent by a legend that a cat had bravely protected the baby Jesus from rats and snakes. But in the end, the old image prevailed.

Cats began to stow away on Phoenician ships. Since the Phoenicians were prolific traders with just about everybody in the ancient world, this had the effect of strengthening the cat population throughout the entire Mediterranean region but, much more importantly, it introduced cats into northern Europe.

At first, things went rather well for them. The Irish and their canny cousins the Scots observed the newcomers carefully and decided that cats were magical creatures with links to the faerie kingdom and much to be admired, respected and, perhaps, even feared. According to Celtic folklore, the Cat Sidhe (Irish) and Cat Sith (Scots) were faeries in the form of large black cats with a single white spot on the chest who mainly haunted the Scottish highlands. The Scandinavians went a step further and associated them with the goddess Freya: in Norse mythology they are pictured as drawing her chariot, thus showing them to be her faithful servants.

But these were the days when something very nasty was about to happen throughout Europe, eerily foreshadowed by a creeping Celtic belief that the Cat Sidhe/Cat Sith was not a true faerie at all, but a shape-shifting witch with the power to adopt feline form a total of nine times.

The Cat and the Broomstick

During the late fifteenth century, a workman found himself under attack by a large cat while chopping firewood for his home in the diocese of Strasbourg. He dodged the raking claws and was in the process of fighting it off when a second, even larger, cat appeared to join the first in its attack. When he attempted to drive them away, he found himself assaulted by a third, all three jumping at his face and biting and scratching his legs.

Understandably, he began to panic. He dropped his axe and threw himself on the cats, which were now swarming over his woodpile, using it as a launch pad for attacks on his head and throat. It took considerable effort, fuelled by desperation, but he finally drove them away by beating one on the head, another on the legs and the third on the back. Then he took a moment to catch his breath, made sure there was no sign of the cats returning and went back to chopping wood.

About an hour later, two men appeared, introduced themselves as servants of the local magistrate and told him they had orders to take him into custody. They escorted him into town and led him to the judge. Like a story from Kafka, the judge kept his distance, refusing to divulge under what charge the woodsman was being held, or listen to his protestations of innocence. Worse still, he ordered him thrown into the deepest dungeon of a prison tower traditionally reserved for those under sentence of death.

For three days, the man kept up a barrage of complaints to his guards, all the time protesting his innocence of any crime. The men were sympathetic, but each time they approached the judge for a hearing, he became angry and indignant that the prisoner refused to acknowledge his crime in the face of all the evidence against him. There was still no indication of what the evidence might be.

But where the guards failed, the judge's fellow magistrates prevailed and the woodsman was eventually granted a hearing. The prisoner was released from his cell and escorted into court. The judge refused even to look at him, but the woodsman threw himself on his knees before the other magistrates and pleaded that he should be told the reason for his arrest.

At this point, the judge finally broke his silence: 'You most wicked of men, how can you not acknowledge your crime? You beat three respected matrons of this town so that they lie in their beds unable to rise or move.'

The woodsman protested that he had never beaten a woman in his life and, when told the precise day and hour of his alleged crime, offered to provide credible witnesses to the fact that he had been chopping wood at the time – and had still been doing so when the judge's servants came for him.

His protestations sent the judge into a fury. 'See how he tries to conceal his crime! The women are bewailing their blows. They exhibit the marks and publicly testify that he struck them.'

The prisoner thought about this for a moment then blurted, 'I remember that I struck some creatures at that time, but they were not women.' When the magistrates questioned him further, he told them the whole story about the cats.

Today, his tale would be dismissed as fantasy or lies, but in the fifteenth century it was accepted at face value and assumed to be the work of witchcraft. The magistrates

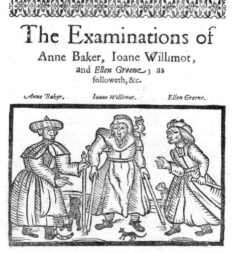

The Examinations of

Anne Baker, Ioane Willimot,
and *Ellen Greene*; as
followeth, &c.

Anne Baker.　　　*Ioane Willimot.*　　　*Ellen Greene.*

*Image from a contemporary report on the witch trials
of the seventeenth century.*

would typically have supposed the cats were devils or at the very least witches who had transformed themselves into feline shape. The injured women might be thought of as collateral damage when the witches magically transferred the beating they were getting (as cats) to three innocent victims. Or, if the women had a poor local reputation, they might be accused of being the witches themselves. In any case, the woodsman was released unharmed, with a warning to tell no one of the whole sorry affair.

The story is drawn from an unusual source, the *Malleus Maleficarum* ('The Hammer of Witches'), described, with reason, as one of the most blood-soaked literary works in human history. The *Malleus* was written in the late fifteenth century by two Dominican clerics, Heinrich Kramer and Jacob Sprenger.[*] Their purpose was to establish the existence of witchcraft – practised mainly by women – and to record the procedures by which a witch might be discovered. They succeeded admirably for it quickly became a guidebook for Inquisition prosecutors, and despite being condemned by the Catholic Church as early as 1490, it continued to be used by royal courts during the Renaissance and contributed to the persecution of accused witches during the sixteenth and seventeenth centuries. The introduction to one modern on-line edition of the work reports that it held at least some responsibility for a worldwide death toll estimated

[*] Or possibly just Kramer: there is scholarly disagreement about the exact authorship.

to range from six hundred thousand to nine million, almost all women.

It started innocently enough. In 1231, Pope Gregory IX set up a Papal Inquisition. His initial targets were the Waldensians and Cathars, two sects who sinned deeply by leading lives of Christ-like simplicity, but eventually the Inquisition's remit was extended to take in a long list of heresies, including sodomy, polygamy, blasphemy, usury and, later, witchcraft.

At first the Inquisition was simply a new method of trial. The old ecclesiastical court system was replaced by single officials – inquisitors – with the authority to demand information from anyone they wished and, if necessary, take action if heresy came to light. An inquisitor's powers were limited in the maximum punishment he could impose; a simple penance was often the most that was allowed. But Gregory IX died in 1241 and in 1243 a new pope, Innocent IV, authorised the use of torture.

On 22 August 1320, a papal bull was issued laying the foundations of the witch hunts that were to sweep across Europe. It specifically authorised a French inquisitor to investigate all those who used images or sacred objects to make magic and those who worshipped or made pacts with demons. The first sorcery trial was held in Carcassonne just a decade after the bull. Five years later, Inquisitor Bernardus Guidonis condemned eight defendants to the stake, one on the basis of her confession that she had learned the secrets of evil from a goat. By 1350, the Inquisition had tried more than a thousand French citizens for sorcery and burned at least half of them.

The use of torture (or 'advanced interrogation techniques', as we like to call it nowadays) had some interesting consequences. One was that defendants would confess to anything.* Another was that, as confessions became more and more imaginative, witches developed a fearsome reputation.

I've known a good few witches in my day and never met one I didn't like. In most cases, they've been sweet, kind, generous, intelligent and attractive women with not a bad thought in their heads. But the picture that emerges from Inquisition trial records across Europe in the Dark Ages is very different. With their feet burned off in charcoal braziers,† witches admitted to personal contact with the Devil himself, to the wholesale murder of babies, to membership of a sort of far-flung magical Mafia, to attendance at Black Masses known as sabbats and to the use of broomsticks in a naughty way.‡ 'So heinous are the crimes of witches,' wrote Kramer and Sprenger in their *Malleus Maleficarum*, 'that they even exceed the sins and the fall of the bad Angels.' People believed them. As a result, witches came to be greatly feared indeed.

And so, it transpired, did their cats. Part of the reason was the old Greek myth of Galinthias.

---

* You don't think she *really* learned the secrets of evil from a goat, do you?
† And the charred bones presented to them in a little bag as a souvenir.
‡ Hint: it wasn't for flying.

Cats' Lowest Hour

The old Greek myth of Galinthias told how Zeus, king of the gods, seduced the Princess Alcmene so successfully that she became pregnant with the hero Heracles. Zeus's wife, Hera, was understandably jealous and sent her daughter Eileithyia (who happened to be the goddess of childbirth) to delay delivery so that, according to astrological predictions, Heracles would be born a girl and thus quite useless for heavy work, like cleaning stables or slaying hydras.

Eileithyia stationed herself outside Alcmene's bedroom, sitting with legs crossed and fingers interlaced to hold them together – a well-known spell for postponing childbirth. The spell worked like a charm until Alcmene's servant, Galinthias, stuck her oar in by announcing loudly that the baby had been born. Eileithyia was so startled that she unclasped her fingers. The spell promptly broke and out popped a male Heracles, ready for action.

Now we come to the point of the story. Hera was so furious her plan had been foiled that she turned Galinthias into a cat and banished her to the underworld to serve Hecate, the Greek goddess of witchcraft, ghosts and dark magic.

This, of course, gave the imprimatur of classical tradition to a link between cats and witchcraft. By one of those weird coincidences history sometimes throws up, the Hecate myth fitted in rather nicely with another belief held in inquisitorial circles at the time. This was the notion that after witches kissed the Devil's bottom, he gave each of them an imp to help them with their badness. Known as *familiars*, these imps manifested as small animals – rats, dogs, squirrels, rabbits and the like. At least, that was how they used to manifest. As the Greek legend gained wider and wider acceptance, witches' familiars came to be identified almost exclusively with cats, usually given spooky names like Pyewacket and Griselda Grizzleguts.

Cats' association with witchcraft turned out to be a huge disaster. The Church went from condemning the witches to condemning the witches and everything associated with them – including their feline familiars. Thus cats were linked directly with the Devil. A superstitious population came to believe their flesh was poisonous and their breath caused consumption.

You can't get much worse than that and while the Inquisition had to go to the trouble and expense of bringing accused witches to trial, no such constraints applied to witches' familiars. Before long people took to slaughtering cats whenever they could get their hands on them. Cat populations plunged.

This could well have marked the end of cats' long friendship with humanity, but in the event, the cats found an unlikely ally in the form of a bacterium called *Yersinia pestis*.

In 1346, *Yersinia pestis* stormed out of the Eurasian steppe like a Mongol horde and roared down the Silk Road in their millions, leaving a trail of devastation in their wake. They were first called the 'Blue Sickness' but later attracted a more pungent – and accurate – epithet as the Black Death. The disease reached Europe in October 1348 and took just two years to wipe out a third of the continent's population, an estimated 75 million people. At the time, it was widely ascribed to the wrath of God. Later, people discovered the real culprit was the black rat.

Unlike common brown rats, which like to hide themselves away in sewers and cellars, black rats prefer to snuggle up with people in nice warm houses. Which is all very well until the rats become infected with the Black Death. It takes roughly ten to fourteen days for the plague to kill off the bulk of an infected rat colony, setting off a very unfortunate chain reaction.

Black rats carry fleas. As an infected colony dies off, the fleas on the dead rats first migrate to the remaining live rats, but are eventually faced with a situation in which there just aren't enough rats to go round. Fleas begin to starve in greater and greater numbers. After about three hungry days, they turn to humans for fresh supplies of blood.

But, hungry or not, every flea that jumps ship to a human has recently been feeding on infected rat blood and consequently suffers from a massive build-up of *Yersinia pestis* in its throat, usually resulting in a partial blockage. When the flea starts to feed on a human, the blockage causes it to vomit blood — and a hefty collection of *Yersinia pestis* bacteria – into the bite site. From there, the contagion drains to the victim's lymph nodes in his groin, thighs, armpits and neck. Overwhelmed by the virulent nature of the disease, the nodes swell into painful suppurating lumps known as *buboes*.

The infection typically incubates for anything up to five days before the buboes appear and the victim feels ill. After that, it takes a further three to five days for him to die – at least in 80 per cent of cases. But that's only the typical timescale. There are cases on record of people waking fit as a flea in the morning only to be dead by sunset.

Everybody had their own ideas about the cause. By far the most popular was that the Black Death was divine punishment for humanity's sins. The Church held spectacular penitential processions and priests were called more often than doctors when someone fell ill.* Cat-lovers have their own ideas about what was

* It took a further two hundred years and a fresh outbreak of plague for a doctor to come up with an effective treatment. His name was Nostradamus. Yes, *that* Nostradamus. He was famous as a plague doctor long before he became known as a prophet. He also owned a cat called Grimalkin.

going on. They point out that you can't spend decades trying to eradicate cats without ecological consequences: in this case more rats. More rats, more fleas, more fleas, more plague. Right up to the present day there are cat-hating academics who reject this argument, but the logic seems sound to me. In any case, the facts are that, after a few terrifying epidemics, people stopped being so beastly to cats, their numbers recovered and we haven't had a major outbreak of the Black Death since.

Cats still had a way to go to achieve their former status, of course, but by the eighteenth century there were a few encouraging signs. In his *Life of Johnson*, for example, the good doctor's biographer, James Boswell, recorded:

I never shall forget the indulgence with which he treated Hodge, his cat: for whom he himself used to go out and buy oysters, lest the servants having that trouble should take a dislike to the poor creature . . . I recollect him one day scrambling up Dr Johnson's breast, apparently with much satisfaction, while my friend smiling and half-whistling, rubbed down his back, and pulled him by the tail; and when I observed he was a fine cat, saying, 'Why yes, Sir, but I have had cats whom I liked better than this;' and then as if perceiving Hodge to be out of countenance, adding, 'but he is a very fine cat, a very fine cat indeed.'

This reminds me of the ludicrous account which he gave . . . of the despicable state of a young Gentleman of good family. 'Sir, when I heard of him last, he was running about town shooting cats.' And then in a sort of kindly reverie, he bethought himself of his own favourite cat, and said, 'But Hodge shan't be shot; no, no, Hodge shall not be shot.'

Hodge wasn't shot, of course. In fact, London eventually erected a statue to him outside the house where he used to live with Dr Johnson at 17 Gough Square. It was unveiled by the lord mayor, Sir Richard Nichols, in 1997.

But it was more than a century after Hodge's lifetime before cats generally began to regain anything like their original high status. Ironically, it came about largely due to Ancient Egypt. There was a lot of archaeological excavation going on in Egypt during the nineteenth century, much of it widely reported in the British newspapers. Readers lapped up exotic stories about the ancient worship of cats and the sacred images of the goddess Bast. Among those readers was Queen Victoria, who appears to have been particularly interested in a perceived feline connection with monarchy: Bast was divine, and the Queen firmly believed the British monarchy was divinely appointed.

Victoria's interest peaked with her acquisition from a Miss Patterson of two Blue Persians with whom she fell passionately in love – so much so that she decided the pair warranted the status of full members of the royal court. The papers got hold of the story and their readers quickly decided that what was good enough for the Queen was good enough for them. Suddenly, everybody who was anybody wanted a cat of their own to love and cherish. Among them was Charles Dickens, the most popular novelist of his day, and Lewis Carroll, who created perhaps the most enduring fictional feline, the Cheshire Cat, famous for vanishing in stages until only his grin was left.

What was the Cheshire Cat grinning about? Perhaps it was the article in *Godey's Lady's Book* that carried Victorian fancy for cats across the Atlantic and made the arrogant little beasts popular throughout America by associating them with love and virtue. Perhaps it was news that the world's first cat show was to be held at London's Crystal Palace in 1871, establishing categories[*] that remain in use to this day. Perhaps it was the discovery that some cat-owners had taken to having clothes specially made for their pets in order to preserve their modesty.

For the next century or so, cats concentrated on building up their numbers and succeeded admirably. Today, there are an estimated 600 million of them wandering the planet, the vast majority of which have human servants to look after them. They have achieved their ambition to become the world's most popular pet.

[*] No pun intended.

In the States, house cats outnumber dogs, their nearest rivals, by a healthy five million margin, a situation mirrored, with varying statistics, worldwide. A 2008 survey by the World Society for the Protection of Animals set figures of 9.8 million cats (6.7 million dogs) in the UK, similar figures for Italy and Poland, 7.8 million cats (5.2 million dogs) in Germany, while the imbalance between cats and dogs is even more extreme in Switzerland, which is home to 1.4 million of the former and fewer than half a million of the latter.[*]

Can this amazing success story really be due to nothing more than a few attractive features and a talent for catching mice? These factors may have played a part, but we must search further for the complete answer, perhaps pushing beyond the part played by cats in civilised times to examine the relationship between cats and men in more primitive cultures. It is a search that will eventually take us into the depths of prehistory . . .

But first it will introduce us to the strangest, most mysterious, perhaps even weirdest, cat of them all.

[*] http://pets.thenest.com/number-dogs-cats-households-world-wide-8973.html Accessed November 2015.

Alien Big Cats

There was something nasty roaming the hilly moorland outside the sleepy little Devon town of South Molton. Since the early 1970s, there had been persistent reports that a phantom black cat had taken residence in the area. Now, in 1983, the reports took on a distinctly sinister edge when a local sheep farmer admitted to the loss of a hundred of his flock over a period of just three months. In each case their throats had been slashed from ear to ear.

The press quickly got hold of the story, christened the phantom the 'Beast of Exmoor' and in one case offered a substantial reward for proven movie footage of the creature. But all that emerged was a young witness who claimed she had seen something black with a long tail and white patches on each foot.[*]

Despite lack of evidence, the government sent a small contingent of Royal Marine snipers into the hills to hunt for the phantom. They remained for three nights, but

[*] https://psmag.com/the-mystery-of-britain-s-alien-big-cats-8cecc4d709ea#.tpvrma6j0

called off the search for fear of shooting one of the photographers now swarming across the area in the hope of earning the newspaper reward.

The fuss died down eventually. The sheep killings stopped. The Beast of Exmoor, like so many of its kind, passed into the myth and mystery that is the Alien Big Cat.

It isn't a house cat. It isn't a native wildcat. It isn't a jungle cat. It is a cat so strange, so controversial that – like the yeti of Tibet or Sasquatch of North America – its very existence has often been officially denied. It is the ABC or Alien Big Cat. And it deserves our attention not only because it seems to share our living space but also because it bridges the gap between natural phenomenon and the downright uncanny, making it perhaps the most mysterious denizen of our mysterious world of cats.

Alien Big Cats are large felines that turn up in places far from their natural habitats. Sightings have been reported in Britain, the United States, Italy, Luxembourg, Spain, Ireland, Finland, Denmark, Canada, New Zealand and Australia. They are typically described as black and about the size of a leopard, though they can be grey, brown or white, and sightings of cats as big as lions have sometimes been reported.

Like Bigfoot and the Loch Ness Monster, they have been captured on camera, but the images are so often indistinct that some cryptozoologists have speculated on the possibility of a supernatural element in their nature. There is, however, nothing supernatural about the tracks they leave, not to mention claw marks on trees and the remains of occasional kills.

Perhaps the oldest reports of ABCs originated some two hundred years ago on the Sunshine Coast of Queensland, Australia, although witness accounts were met with scepticism at the time. There is controversy of a different sort surrounding the Tantanoola Tiger, another Australian sighting. Any doubts about the reality of the creature were laid to rest in 1895 when it was shot, stuffed and mounted for display in a local hotel. But there remain doubts about the nature of the beast. Local experts identified it as an Assyrian Wolf, a species of which I can find no record whatsoever. We are perhaps on more stable ground with the Blue Mountains Panther. Sightings in the region west of Sydney have been reported for more than a century and locals simply assume there really are big cats in the area, perhaps descended from zoo and/or circus escapees.

Experts frequently question the reality of Alien Big Cats and the credibility of witnesses. A group of seven professionals called in to examine video footage of a typical panther-style sighting near Lithgow, New South Wales, came to the remarkable conclusion that they were looking at a domestic cat 'two or three times normal size'. More reasonable conclusions have been reached in other Australian cases. In 2003, the New South Wales state government issued a report stating it was 'more likely than not' that a colony of Alien Big Cats was living wild in the bush near Sydney. Another study by Deakin

University was even more definite. It concluded that the existence of big cats in Australia's Grampian Mountains had been 'demonstrated beyond reasonable doubt.'

Alien Big Cat sightings in the United States have to be treated with caution since the country has its own indigenous big cats roaming their natural ranges. Nonetheless, there are a great many reliable sightings that appear to fall into the 'Phantom Cat' classification.

ABC stories have circulated in Hawaii, for example, since the 1980s and attracted attention from the authorities when there was a substantial jump in the number of reported sightings during the run-up to Christmas in 2002. The Division of Forestry and Wildlife called in two wildlife biologists, who concluded that the mystery cat was possibly a leopard illegally imported into the islands as a pet, then released. But while sightings continued to be reported, attempts to catch the cat with the aid of traps, infrared cameras and professional trackers all proved futile and the hunt was called off in late 2003 after a period of three weeks with no reported sightings.

Black panther sightings are common across California, particularly in the aptly named Mount Diablo region of Contra Costa County. Accounts of the same beasts are also common in North Carolina while the Delaware Division of Fish and Wildlife accepts that there may be a small population of mountain lions in the county's northern forests, bred from animals released from captivity.

Rather more mysterious are the reports originating from countries with no history of indigenous big-cat populations. In 1995, newspapers in Denmark reported on what they called the Beast of Funen, a lion seen by numerous eyewitnesses. Another lion was spotted – again by numerous witnesses – along the Finnish–Russian border in the summer of 1992. A Finnish government biologist was appointed to investigate examined tracks left by the beast and confirmed it was a large feline not native to Finland. An official hunt was mounted by the Ministry of the Interior, but without success, possibly because the lion crossed the border into Russia where it left tracks in an area of raked sand used by Russian border guards to detect intruders.

Even more unexpectedly the little Duchy of Luxembourg played host to a black panther in 2009. There was no trace of the beast when police arrived in the industrial area where it was sighted, but it was spotted again by various witnesses across the country during the following few days. A local zoo denied that any of their panthers was missing and the entire incident was subsequently explained away as a misidentification of a particularly large house cat.*

But perhaps the most interesting of all ABC territories is Britain, where sightings date back to the eighteenth century and alien big cats have actually been captured or shot.

* All ABC reports sourced in September 2016 from http://en.wikipedia.org/wiki/Gippsland_phantom_cat

British ABCs

Twenty-six-year-old hotel worker Nich Boden was walking home from a friend's house on the night of 9 July 2015, when he was attacked so ferociously in a stretch of remote woodland between Coniston and Hawkshead (Westmorland) that he did not even see his assailant before he was knocked unconscious to the ground.

When he awoke minutes later, all he could remember was being struck violently from in front and to the right. There was no longer any sign of his attacker, but Boden was left with a deep gouge on his shoulder and claw marks on his forearm. It was clear he had been savaged by a wild animal of some sort, but those claw marks were something of a mystery. They looked like cat scratches, but they were too far apart to have been inflicted by any cat smaller than a lion.

There were no reports of lion escapes from zoos or circuses in the area, but when Boden contacted the local paper he discovered there had been a sighting of an alien big cat in the district just the week before . . .

In 2004, the British Big Cats Society completed a survey of 2,052 reported sightings of alien big cats across the United Kingdom. Statistical analysis located nine per cent of these in the West Midlands, 11 per cent in Scotland, 12 per cent in East Anglia, 16 per cent in south-east England and 21 per cent in south-west England.[*] Although eyewitness descriptions varied widely in terms of size and colour, the typical report was of a black cat as big as a German Shepherd dog.[†]

The earliest known reference to an alien big cat in Britain dates back to the mid-thirteenth century and appears in a Welsh poem entitled '*Pa Gwr*' forming part of the *Black Book of Carmarthen*. The medieval text tells of a mysterious cat, Cath Palug, that terrorised Anglesey until slain by a local hero. In true mythic style, the cat was identified as the offspring of a monstrous pig called Henwen.

The earliest eyewitness account was reported in the eighteenth century by the writer William Cobbett, who recalled a visit to the ruins of Waverley Abbey near Farnham in Surrey during his childhood. While walking in the grounds, he saw a cat, which he later described as 'big as a middle-sized Spaniel dog', climb into a hollow elm tree. He had no idea what it was at the time but years later in New Brunswick he saw a North American Lynx and immediately recognised it as the

* *Ibid.*
† *Fortean Times*, 344, September 2016.

same species of animal that he had seen as a boy in Waverley. If so, it was not the only lynx to roam the British countryside. One was shot in Devon in 1903, with its remains now preserved in the Bristol Museum.

Since then, there has been an apparently endless series of alien-big-cat sightings throughout the country. In one year alone, a British research group reported 89 in Leicestershire, 91 in Somerset, 92 in Kent, 99 in Cornwall, 103 in Sussex, 104 in Gloucestershire, 123 throughout Wales, 125 in Scotland, 127 in Yorkshire and 132 in Devon. Although the numbers seem high, they represent only a top ten by county or district, not a national total. Furthermore, it is probably safe to say that many more sightings failed to be recorded anywhere prior to the late 1950s when print media finally discovered that giving an ABC a dramatic name made for a good story. A favourite ploy was to link the location of the sighting with the name of any old cat, irrespective of whether it matched eyewitness descriptions or not – hence reports of a 'Surrey Puma' and 'Fen Tiger'.

By the 1970s, some sharp-witted journalist realised a term like *beast* sounded far more threatening and exciting than simple *cat*, hence the media appearance of the Beast of Exmoor, following multiple sightings of an ABC in Devon and Somerset. The power of alliteration made itself felt in 1992 when the Beast of Bodmin created headlines across the country. There were so many sightings of a panther-like creature concentrated on Bodmin Moor in Cornwall that the suspicion arose of the existence of a breeding colony, rather than a single big cat.

So persistent were the rumours that, in 1995, the Ministry of Agriculture, Fisheries and Food was moved to publish the results of an official investigation that concluded, 'No verifiable evidence for the presence of a big cat was found,' and consequently 'There is no significant threat to livestock from a big cat in Bodmin Moor.'

But there was a weird addendum to the story. Only days after publication of the ministry's report, a young boy was out walking by the banks of the River Fowey, a waterway that has its main source on Bodmin Moor, when he found the skull of a big cat. The size of the skull and, in particular, its prominent canines, suggested it had belonged to a leopard. It looked as if the ministry had given up on its search for evidence just a little too soon.

The Natural History Museum in London verified that the skull was indeed that of a leopard. But there were several mysteries surrounding the find. First, there were indications that the flesh had not rotted in the usual way, but been scraped from the bone with a knife. Then there was the fact that the back of the skull had been cut off cleanly using some unknown instrument. There were signs of decomposition, but experts determined that this had begun quite recently, after the skull had been immersed in water. Finally, museum scientists discovered a tropical cockroach eggshell inside the skull itself. Piecing the various clues together, the museum investigators concluded that the leopard had not died on Bodmin Moor, but its remains had been imported as a leopard-skin rug.

Meanwhile, reports of living British big cats continued to pour in. Gloucestershire police alone logged seventy-five during the six years from 2005. In 2011, the Beast of Dartmoor – a large black panther – made an appearance in Haldon Forest, witnessed by a group of no fewer than fifteen people. During the same year, another panther was spotted numerous times by eyewitnesses in the Shotts, North Lanarkshire, district.

The year 2012 began with a bumper crop of sightings. ABCs were seen in Westmorland, Herefordshire, Shropshire, Somerset and Kent. There were press reports of a 'Calderdale Catbeast', following the discovery of an enormous paw print in West Yorkshire. There were further paw prints found in the Mendip Hills and South Chailey, while a black panther was chased out of a house in East Sussex. By March, an alien big cat had been photographed in Hereford. The following month, more paw prints turned up near Peterborough.

In May, things took on a distinctly darker tinge with the discovery of twenty dead and mutilated sheep at the aptly named Devil's Bridge in the Cambrian Mountains near Aberystwyth in Wales. All meat had been stripped from the carcasses, leaving only bones and fleece. Earlier attacks in the same district had led the press to name the culprit as the Beast of Bont.

There was an even more frightening development when summer rolled around. Residents of an Essex caravan park reported sightings of a lion roaming the Clacton-on-Sea district. Confirmation was provided when locals heard the sound of a lion's roar and one eyewitness managed to take a photograph of the beast. The authorities took the reports very seriously. Police advised residents of the area to remain indoors for their own safety and mounted a thorough search of the district as well as contacting zoos and circuses. Nothing was found and there were no reports of an escaped lion. Later in the year, however, two dog walkers saw a lion loose in a Bedford housing estate, a brown big cat was reported in Brockworth, Gloucestershire, while a sandy-coloured ABC was seen picking up fish from a Lincolnshire sea wall.

Alien big cats continued to prowl throughout Britain during 2013. Police received forty-five reports of them throughout the year. Some of those reports were quite spectacular – two cats were seen chasing a small group of deer. Sometimes they turned up in the most unexpected places, like the beast that jumped out in front of Jack Humphrey's car near Wellington in Shropshire or the ABC seen strolling across a Berkshire golf course.

This was the year that marked the sighting of a British big cat followed by the discovery of its lair. The cat was originally seen at night by two sisters on the Shropshire–Wrexham border as it leaped over the fence and disappeared across a field. When they returned in daylight to search the area, they discovered the creature's lair, marked by its paw prints. The prints were too large for a domestic cat, but seemed small for a leopard or panther. An expert who examined them speculated that they might belong to a descendant of a Shropshire jungle cat reported back in the 1980s.

2014 proved notable for the fact that an Essex resident managed to film a black ABC as it prowled near her home in Great Hallingbury. It was also the year of a celebrity sighting. Clare Balding, the well-known British television presenter, reported that she'd seen another black ABC at the Doward beauty spot near Ross-on-Wye in Herefordshire. There were also reports of sheep and deer killings, some associated with direct big-cat sightings and in all cases stripped to the bones of their meat.

As the years roll on, reports of alien big cats in the British countryside show no signs of abating. But 2015 may have set some sort of record for the size of an ABC when a former policewoman saw one she estimated to be about as big as a pony, while attending to horses in a field near Finchingfield in Essex. The year also marked the rare appearance of two alien big cats together. They were sighted at Fressingfield in Suffolk.

Towards the end of the year, the media were busily resurrecting stories about the Beast of Bolton (first sighted in 2006) following reports of an ABC seen from a car near Bolton in Lancashire. It was described as having a long tail, pointed ears and yellow eyes.

ABC reports continued to flood in during 2016. In February there were three sightings in Kent – at

Maidstone, Sevenoaks and Canterbury – within ninety minutes of each other. Seven sightings were recorded in Fife, twelve more in the Lake District, the most recent of forty logged by local police since 2003. More sightings followed in various parts of the country during March and April, while towards the end of June a big cat made its appearance in Winnie the Pooh country at Ashdown Forest, East Sussex.*

So what is going on? Conventional wisdom provides a variety of answers.

Alien big cats don't exist: eyewitnesses are deluded, mistakenly identifying domestic cats as something more exotic or, alternatively, simply making up stories for the sake of a little publicity.

Alien big cats do exist: they are escapees from zoos and circuses or sometimes deliberate releases of exotic big cats into the wild. Alternatively, they are rare examples of exceptionally big domestic cats.

It is true that any of these possibilities might apply – and some certainly do apply – in specific cases. The lion that prowled near the Essex caravan park in 2012 was later claimed to have been identified as Teddy, a pet Maine Coon owned by a local resident. In 2016 a two-year-old Carpathian Lynx named Flaviu chewed his way through a board to escape from his enclosure shortly after transfer to Dartmoor Zoo, occasioning a

* All sightings quoted in this section sourced from http://en.wikipedia.org/wiki/British_big_cats and *Fortean Times*, September 2016.

police search involving helicopters and drones. A former lion-tamer confessed in 2000 to releasing a panther and a cougar in a remote area of the Derbyshire Pennines as long ago as 1974.

But there are problems. The lion-tamer's belated confession goes nowhere to explain literally hundreds of sightings across broad swathes of the British countryside. Cats that escape from zoos, circuses or safari parks are typically reported missing within hours. A Maine Coon is the largest breed of domestic cat. Weighing in at up to eighteen pounds and reaching a record length of more than four feet, nose to tail, it is almost comparable in size to a Eurasian lynx and might well be mistaken for an even bigger cat when glimpsed momentarily by an excitable witness. But the residents of the Essex caravan park heard their big cat roar like a lion. Maine Coons can't roar.

In 1976, Britain's Parliament expressed its concern at the growing numbers of big cats in private ownership across the country by voting through the government's Dangerous Wild Animals Act. The legislation basically allowed legal ownership of a dangerous wild animal, but only under licence – and the cost of such was purposely set extremely high. Critics of the Act complained that one of its consequences might be that current wild-animal owners would simply turn the beasts loose rather than stump up for an expensive licence.

This early criticism has frequently been put forward as an explanation for alien big cats, particularly when groups of sightings come together. But it fails on two main counts. The first is that there are very few big cats in private ownership, whereas reports of ABCs have run into the hundreds – if not perhaps thousands – over the years. Even if every privately owned big cat were to be released at once, it would still not account for current numbers of reported sightings. The second point is even simpler. There were many historical reports of ABCs long before the Dangerous Wild Animals legislation was enacted.

Another complication arises from the fact that, as already mentioned, the typical ABC sighting is of an all-black cat about the size of a leopard. Completely black cats are, in fact, comparatively rare in the wild. The description really only fits a panther. So why, with so many other possible breeds to choose from, is there such a preponderance of 'panthers' roaming around Britain? And perhaps the most intractable problem of all, why cats? Why not alien giraffes or alien gorillas?

It is problems like these with the conventional explanations that have led some people to postulate a paranormal element to ABCs. Certainly paranormal explanations feature commonly in big-cat folklore, as typified by the Tennessee legend of the wampus cat.

The legend concerns a Native American tribe in which the women were forbidden to witness the sacred songs and hunting magic reserved strictly for the men. One day, a beautiful tribeswoman could contain her curiosity no longer and secretly followed her husband on one of his hunting trips with the other men. When the men camped for the night, she hid behind a rock and wrapped the hide of a mountain cat around her for warmth. From this vantage point, she spied on the men as they began their sacred rituals.

Unfortunately for her, she was spotted and captured by one of the younger braves. He brought her at once to the tribe's medicine man, who meted out a dreadful punishment for her breaking of tribal taboos. First he bound her into the mountain-cat skin she was wearing, then worked powerful magic to change her into a monster, half woman, half big cat. He then condemned her to roam the hills for ever, howling pitifully for the return of her normal body.

As in so much folklore of this type, the story does not end there. In an addendum designed to underscore the truth of the legend, we learn of a white hunter out one night with his rifle and two dogs. He had entered the Tennessee hills when the dogs ran off in fright. At once he was assailed by a horrible smell, then heard a howl behind him. The hunter spun round to find himself facing the terrifying wampus cat, a creature that walked upright like a human but had the fangs and glowing yellow eyes of a mountain lion.

The hunter turned tail and ran, the wampus cat close on his heels. He ran for his life until he reached the house of a friend and dived inside. Realising what was happening, the friend slammed the door behind him. But almost at once, it threatened to burst open under the violent attack of the pursuing wampus cat.

The friend realised this was a supernatural creature and reached for his Bible. As he began to read aloud from the Psalms, the attack on the door gradually subsided and, with a final howl of anguish, the great cat withdrew and made its way back into the hills from which it had come.

A legend is, of course, only a legend, but elements of this one may repay closer examination. Notably the fact that at its heart it is primarily concerned with ailuranthropy, a term derived from the Greek referring to the supposed ability of some humans to transform into animals. The most common form of ailuranthrope – in Europe, at least – is the werewolf, but different cultures have their own versions of the myth, hence tales of weretigers in India, wereleopards in Africa and, unexpectedly, werehares in Japan. We have already noted mythological references to this very talent, usually attributed to gods or goddesses.

In the legend of the wampus cat, we have the story of a beautiful Indian woman magically transformed into a cougar, or at least into a monstrous mixture between a cougar and a human. More to the point, we have details of how this transformation came about: the woman was wrapped in the skin of a mountain lion, which the Native American shaman (medicine man) used to trigger the change.

Could these details be a distorted recollection of something real? It seems incredible from our conventional Western perspective, but before making up our minds, it may be useful to consider a curious experience of William Seabrook, the American travel writer.

Seabrook was in a flat overlooking Times Square in New York with a group of people who were experimenting with the *I Ching*, an ancient Chinese oracle sometimes claimed to be the oldest book in the world. To use the oracle, you would normally generate a random six-lined figure called a hexagram, then look up its meaning in the book. But on this occasion the group was using a more occult method: the chosen hexagram was visualised painted on a stout wooden door, which was contemplated in the mind's eye until it opened, allowing the querent to step mentally through.

On the occasion Seabrook recorded, the querent was a Russian émigrée named Magda. It took her nearly twenty minutes to get the imaginal door to open and in doing so she appeared to pass into a trance. To the consternation of her friends, she grew increasingly disturbed, groaning softly and writhing in her chair. Suddenly she called out loudly, 'I'm naked. I'm naked underneath a fur coat. I'm running. I'm running naked in the snow!' Her limbs were jerking spasmodically now and she was making growling noises deep in her throat. When her friends tried to wake her, she lashed out at them furiously and even tried to bite them when they came too close.

Eventually they broke through her trance, and when they did so she explained what had happened. The imaginal doorway in her mind had opened onto a snow-covered landscape, similar to those she remembered from her native Russia. When she stepped through, her humanity slipped quickly away and she found herself transformed into a wolf running joyfully through the snow. She had effectively become a werewolf, although no physical change had occurred.

It is easy to see how stories of Magda's experience might be distorted in the telling until they, too, become transformed. Could the legend of the Tennessee wampus cat be the result of a similar distortion? Is it beyond the bounds of possibility that a real medicine man, perhaps using hypnosis, once persuaded a real tribeswoman she had turned into a cat?

This is a strange, fascinating area for investigation, which may well have a bearing on the mystery of the relationship between cats and the human race. And, as we shall see in our next chapter, that relationship has had some very dark aspects indeed.

The Leopard Men

The most dangerous cat in the wild is not the lordly lion or the terrifying tiger, but the substantially smaller leopard. A herd of elephants that stood firm against a tiger attack was seen to flee at the approach of a single marauding leopard.

Leopards lead a solitary existence. They mark out territories that sometimes overlap but, outside mating, try to keep at least a kilometre apart and will readily attack intruders of the same sex. Like domestic cats, they sleep through most of the day and hunt at night, wandering across their range for anything up to fifteen miles. They are so well camouflaged, so stealthy in their movements and habits, that people often remain unaware they sometimes have leopards as close neighbours.

A leopard can swim as well as a tiger, run at speeds of 36 m.p.h., leap distances of twenty feet and jump vertically as high as ten feet. They are exceptionally good at climbing trees – the only cats I am aware of that can come down again head first – and so strong that they can drag carcasses of their own weight into the upper branches for storage. They will eat almost anything, from insects, like a dung beetle, all the way up to an eland weighing almost a ton. In between, they will cheerfully consume rats and squirrels, porcupines, monkeys, warthogs, themselves (although cannibalism is extremely rare), impala and wildebeest. They especially like the taste of dog, baboon and, once sampled, human.

According to an account in the *Journal of the Bombay Natural History Society*:

> Like the tiger, the leopard sometimes takes to maneating and a man-eating leopard is even more to be dreaded than a tiger with similar tastes, on account of its greater agility, and also its greater stealthiness and silence. It can stalk and jump and can climb better than a tiger and it can also conceal itself in astonishingly meagre cover, often displaying uncanny intelligence in this act. A man-eating leopard frequently breaks through the frail walls of village huts and carries away children and even adults as they lie asleep.

The taste for human flesh is a particularly old one. A six-million-year-old hominid fossil femur found in Kenya displays leopard-teeth marks, while 1.8-million-year-old hominid remains unearthed in South Africa in 1970 showed signs of having been dragged into a tree and eaten by a leopard. Other fossil finds at the site suggested early humans were a favourite prey of prehistoric leopards.

Two million years of evolution has taught leopards to avoid human contact wherever possible, but circumstances arise from time to time that lead to a resurgence of the ancient appetite. One example was the worldwide influenza epidemic of 1918, which was particularly virulent in India. As the death toll mounted, villagers took to throwing the corpses into the jungle rather than giving them a proper burial. Hungry leopards gratefully scavenged the bodies and found they liked what they tasted. When the epidemic finally burned itself out and there were no more flu victims to be eaten, some leopards turned to killing humans. In this way, two Indian man-eaters emerged in the wake of epidemics. Between them, they killed 525 people.

Shocking though that last statistic was, it does not mark either of the two leopards involved as the deadliest man-eater of all time. That doubtful distinction goes to the Panar Leopard, a male living in the Kumaon area of India during the early years of the twentieth century.

The leopard's range was remote, so details of its activities are sparse, but the bare bones of its story seem to be that it was wounded by a poacher, leaving it unable to hunt for normal prey. Like other big cats before it, the Panar Leopard quickly discovered that humans were easier to catch and tasted delicious. No statistics were compiled on its early kills, but eventually the authorities in the Panar province (where the leopard ranged most frequently) sat up, took notice and began to keep records. By the time the beast was shot dead in 1910, it had notched up more than four hundred victims. Add that to the numbers that had gone unrecorded and you can begin to recognise why hunters and other experts consider the leopard to be the smallest but most deadly of all the big cats.

Despite – or possibly because of – this reputation, some tribal communities in Africa have formed an intimate relationship with the beast that borders on the mystical. Typical examples are the Ibibio peoples, who mainly inhabit the Cross River State of south-eastern Nigeria.

The Ibibio are a rainforest people, skilled in wood-carving, who cultivate yams and export palm oil and kernels. Their typical village, inhabited by about five hundred people, consists of rectangular compounds arranged around central courtyards and divided into different wards.

The government of each ward consists of a council made up of the heads of the various households plus a ward leader. But this government is little more than a secular shell. Real power among the Ibibio is vested in the Ekpe, a secret 'Leopard Society' open only to men of good standing and influence; and then only those with sufficient funds to pay substantial initiation fees at its higher levels.

The society was originally founded for magical purposes – the shamanic propitiation of forest spirits for the benefit of the community as a whole. In practice, however, members gradually extended their authority until their organisation had become a legislature enforcing its own laws by means of fines, boycotts and even capital punishment. The society of 'leopard men' judged cases, maintained internal peace and generally functioned as an executive government in its own right. Although its overall power has waned, the society continues to exist into the present day.

An older, darker manifestation of Leopard Society power runs like a bloody thread through Africa's colonial history. Early indications date back to the late 1870s with a series of ritual murders in Libreville, Gabon. The corpses of victims were found beheaded and slashed with giant claw marks, discoveries that spread panic throughout the district since these were ancient signatures of leopard men far less benevolent than those who ran the Ibibio. Throughout the tribal history of West Africa, local cults had often arisen around shamanic beliefs that men could transform themselves into leopards by wearing leopard skins and equipping themselves with steel claws. Transformation generally remained a spiritual practice within the cult, but would occasionally erupt into broader society as cult members sought murderous vengeance on those they considered their enemies.

The Libreville murders continued for three years then stopped for no apparent reason. But only locally. By the 1890s, leopard men were at their grisly work again, this time in Nigeria. By now, colonial authorities were beginning to suspect a political aspect to their activities, and since then analysts have concluded that the spread of leopard-man killings coincided with the spread of colonial power, with the society acting as a focus of guerrilla resistance. Be this as it may, the Leopard Society extended its activities throughout the whole of West Africa, centring itself in Sierra Leone, Liberia, the Ivory Coast and Nigeria.

In a noteworthy development, its members increasingly became man-eaters. Dr Werner Junge, a German physician working in Liberia in the 1930s, left a vivid account of his discovery of one unfortunate victim of this cannibalism:

There, on a mat in a house, I found a horribly mutilated body of a fifteen-year-old girl. The neck was torn to ribbons by the teeth and claws of an animal, the intestines were torn out, the pelvis shattered, and one thigh was missing. A part of the thigh, gnawed to the bone, and a piece of the shinbone lay near the body. It seemed at first glance that only a beast of prey could have treated the girl's body in this way, but closer investigation brought certain peculiarities to light which did not fit in with the picture. I observed, for example, that the skin at the edge of the undamaged part of the chest was torn by strangely regular gashes about an inch long. Also the liver had been removed from the body with the clean cut no beast could make. I was struck, too, by a piece of intestine the ends of which appeared to have been smoothly cut off, and, lastly, there was the fracture of the thigh – a classic example of fracture by bending.*

Note the phrase 'gnawed to the bone' . . .

Note, too, the familiar mixture in all of this: cat, animal skin, shape-shifting, shamanic practice . . . Curiously, it is a mix also found in the mythologies surrounding another of the big cats.

According to fable, the Nemean lion was a semi-magical beast whose golden coat was immune to any weapon. Its purpose in life seems to have been to slay heroes, and it would often abduct beautiful maidens in order to attract heroes to its lair. When the hero reached the lion's cave, he would be met by the sight of the maiden cowering injured and in pain. But when he rushed to her rescue, he quickly discovered this was not the abducted maiden at all. The woman immediately shape-shifted into the Nemean lion, who then attacked and killed the hero, devoured his body and dropped his bones into Hell.

After terrorising the countryside, the Nemean lion finally met its match when its slaughter became one of Heracles' famous twelve labours. At first, the hero tried to shoot it with arrows, but discovered they simply

---

* Werner Junge, *African Jungle Doctor*, Harrap, 1952.

bounced off its magical coat. He then trapped it in its own cave, stunned it with a club and strangled it to death.

The god Zeus was so impressed by this feat that he placed the Nemean lion in the sky as a commemoration. You can see it there to this day in its current manifestation as the constellation Leo.

It is easy to miss what may be a telling detail in the ancient myth of the Nemean lion. After Heracles strangled the beast, he attempted to skin it, forgetting that its pelt was impervious to harm. When the knife in his belt failed to do the trick, he sharpened it on a stone, but to no avail. Then he used the stone itself, again without result. Eventually, inspired by a message from the gods, he managed to skin the lion using one of its own claws.

Why was Heracles so determined to remove the pelt of the Nemean lion? The fable suggests he thought it might make excellent armour, but is that all there was to it?

A point often missed in the excitement of the tale is that the Nemean lion was a shape-shifter. It habitually transformed itself into a beautiful maiden to lure heroes into its lair. Was this the quality of the lion's skin that attracted Heracles, rather than its impervious nature? Did he wish to wear it in order to transform himself into an even more fearsome warrior, half man, half lion? If so, we seem to have wandered back into the same shamanic twilight that we found in the legend of the wampus cat.

Curiously, another of the great cats, the tiger, also has strong mythological associations with shape-shifting. The writer Sharon Guynup draws on 'various fables' to provide this particularly vivid description of the process:

It usually began with the feet turning into enormous paws, equipped with sharp, sheathed claws. Legs and arms, chest and back expanded, rippled with muscle, and then the skin was blanketed in russet fur, slashed by black stripes. A tail appeared between the man-cat's long rear legs. Finally, an enormous tiger head appeared. Back in human form, these people appeared normal, except for one tell-tale physical anomaly: They lacked a groove in their upper lip.*

The broad resemblance between this description and that of the wampus cat is obvious. But there is a pattern forming here that goes far beyond a passing similarity with a North American legend. Where Europe had its werewolf, werecats were the significant shape-shifters throughout most of the rest of the world. In Africa, as we have seen, the legend manifested in tales of werelions and wereleopards, but throughout Asia the were-cat of mythic choice was almost always the weretiger.

What lay behind the shape-shifting varied from legend to legend and place to place. In India, the

* http://voices.nationalgeographic.com/2014/04/09/why-have-tigers-been -feared-and-revered-throughout-history/

weretiger was generally considered to be an evil sorcerer using his powers to prey on livestock and sometimes even human beings. In China, by contrast, the were-tiger was seen more as a victim than a perpetrator, condemned to shape-shift by a family curse or the actions of a malevolent ghost.

There is a close legendary linkage between weretigers and man-eaters. In Thailand, the prevalent myth actually holds that a tiger that eats enough people will become human itself, thereafter transforming at will from man-eater to man. A less extreme – and more benign – version of the same legend suggests that the soul of anyone eaten by a tiger passes into the beast, turning it into a weretiger that will henceforth become a guardian of humans and their interests.

The methods of transformation from man to tiger are also varied. Some legends hold that spells may be used; others insist that shape-shifting is the result of a sort of yoga practice involving fasting and willpower. Here again we have an association with shamanism so that it comes as no surprise to learn shamans in many Asian countries invoke tigers to help them move between the worlds and communicate with spirits. A clue to how this may be achieved is embodied in Hindu religious art where the great god Shiva is portrayed enfolded in a tiger skin. The same thought process is, perhaps, reflected in the Bagh Jatra, a Nepalese tiger festival, during which celebrants dress themselves in tiger costumes and act out typical tiger behaviour in the form of a dance.

According to North American legend, the shape-shifting wampus cat was created using the skin of a mountain lion. According to classical mythology, the hero Heracles worked hard – and, incidentally, risked his life – to obtain the skin of a shape-shifting lion. Traditional Hindu art portrays Shiva as wearing a tiger skin when he shape-shifts into physical manifestation. Legends of shape-shifting cats, big and small, appear in the folklore of many, many different lands – even where there is no obvious communication between them. And everywhere there are mysterious, tenacious hints of shamanic practice. Even the apparently innocent folk festival in Nepal exhibits shamanic elements: part of a shaman's regular practice is to mimic a spirit animal in a magical dance.

Is it possible this pattern – cat, animal skin, shape-shifting, shamanism – may contain a clue to our mysteriously close relationship with domestic cats? If so, our investigations seem to have led us into eldritch territory indeed. But, eldritch or not, now may be the time to take a deep breath and find out more about shamanism.

The Shamanic Worldview

Shamanism is humanity's oldest religion. It teaches that reality is divided into three worlds — the Upper, Middle and Lower. The Upper World is a spiritual realm where you might meet with higher beings, like gods, guides and angels. The Middle World is our familiar physical reality where you stride into the jungle to hunt for game or catch a train to get to the office. The Lower World is home to animal spirits.

Of course, there are all sorts of religions that teach all sorts of nonsense, which doesn't mean any of it is true. Just the same, shamans often claim extraordinary powers and many tribal communities take them seriously. As a consequence of his profession, the shaman must be supported by the community, which considers his professional activity useful, indeed even necessary, for the common good.

The problem that arises is why, if you insist that the shaman's abilities are fictitious, the community should consider his professional activities of any value at all. Yet shamanic prestige is typically so high that far more than minimal support is offered. Among the Evenki of

Russia and China, for example, the shaman is automatically awarded the best stretch of river fishing; he is helped with reindeer herding and is offered frequent gifts of food and furs. It is the absolute duty of every tribal member to aid him economically. For many peoples – among them the Tungus and Samoyed of Siberia, and the northern circumpolar Inuit – the post of shaman and tribal chieftain are one and the same.

The mystery deepens when you look into the history of shamanism. The practice flourished in the bitter extremes of the Ice Age when the borderline between survival and extinction was razor thin. Tribes living in such conditions can't afford passengers.

Our present world is warmer, but shamans are still active in places where the living is far from easy. Conditions in the Kalahari, the Australian outback, the Siberian steppe and the Alaskan Arctic are so hostile that most Europeans would find it impossible to survive there without supply lines and back-up. Yet here, as in many other harsh environments, the shaman practises his craft as he has done for forty thousand years. If he really is a charlatan, you would have thought somebody might have found him out by now.

So what has all this got to do with cats? The thing is, shamans claim they gain their powers from visiting the spirit worlds. If the powers are genuine, and they certainly seem to be, maybe we should be taking spirit worlds a bit more seriously. Is there a possibility they might be real?

At first glance, the evidence isn't promising. Report after report from respected anthropologists tells us that when a shaman 'visits the spirit world', he goes nowhere at all but simply falls into a trance, often smashed out of his skull on botanical hallucinogenics. He may be tripping, like my friends in the sixties, and you would be hard put to imagine his visions were anything more than dreamscapes, but is this an accurate interpretation of the facts?

In 1959, an anthropologist named Michael Harner was invited by the American Museum of Natural History to undertake a field study of the Conibo, a forest people living beside the Peruvian Amazon. Harner agreed, the Conibo proved friendly, but the study didn't go smoothly. Even after a year, Harner found his hosts reluctant to discuss

Shape-shifting cat.

their religious beliefs, the supernatural or their magical practices. Eventually he was told that if he really wished to learn, he would have to imbibe a sacred drink made from a plant called the 'soul vine'. He was warned, however, that this could lead to a very frightening experience. Today, the soul vine is better known by its botanical name, ayahuasca, but Harner's account, untainted by subsequent theories and assumptions, remains one of the best introductions to a fascinating, if still largely mysterious, aspect of human experience. There is nothing in it directly related to cats, but their relevance will become clear later. This then is how Harner described what happened to him.

A Conibo elder named Tomás collected enough ayahuasca and cawa leaves to fill a fifteen-gallon pot and boiled them all afternoon until only about a quart of dark green liquid was left. This he bottled and left to cool.

As night fell, the Conibo muzzled their dogs and instructed the children of the village to be quiet since any intrusive sounds could harm the mind of a person who has drunk ayahuasca. In the firelight, Harner was offered a gourd containing about a third of the bottle of liquid. He felt, he says,* like Socrates accepting the hemlock, but drank it.

Lying on a bamboo platform under the thatched roof of the communal house, he became slowly aware of faint traceries of light that burst into brilliant colours, then the distant sound of a waterfall that grew increasingly

* In *The Way of the Shaman*, HarperSanFrancisco, 1980, Kindle edition, 2011.

strong until it filled his ears. Overhead the faint lines became brighter and gradually interlaced to form a canopy resembling a geometric mosaic of stained glass. He described the experience as follows:

> The bright violet hues formed an ever-expanding roof above me. Within this celestial cavern, I heard the sound of water grow louder and I could see dim figures engaged in shadowy movements. As my eyes seemed to adjust to the gloom, the moving scene resolved itself into something resembling a huge fun house, a super-natural carnival of demons. In the centre, presiding over the activities and looking directly at me, was a gigantic, grinning crocodilian head, from whose cavernous jaws gushed a torrential flood of water.°

Visions of two strange boats followed, combining to form a sort of Viking longship with a square sail. He became conscious of the sound of singing, the most beautiful he had ever heard. He saw bird-headed people on the longship, like the gods of Ancient Egypt.

As predicted, the experience became frightening. Harner felt his soul was being drawn from his body to be carried away on the boat. As this happened, a sort of numbness crept through him, as if he were turning to stone. It required an enormous effort to keep his heart beating and he became convinced he was going to die.

* *Ibid.*

As the conviction increased, he found he was in communication with giant reptilian dragon creatures, shiny and black with short pterodactyl-like wings and huge whale bodies. They had, they explained, come from outer space and had flown to Earth to escape an enemy. It was they who had created the myriad of terrestrial life-forms in order to hide themselves. Thus they now lived in everything, including humanity, and could communicate from the depths of the human mind.

Certain he was now only moments from death, Harner managed to ask the Conibo for medicine and they hurried to prepare an antidote, which eased his condition but did not stop the visions. He seemed to travel beyond the galaxy and conversed with grinning demons.

Harner's experience ended in sleep, and when he awoke, the visions had ended. Despite his scientific training, what had happened seemed so real that he considered himself in grave peril because the dragon creatures had revealed information reserved for those about to die. He began to talk about it to anyone who would listen, on the premise that sharing the information might make it less dangerous to him.

Among those he told were two American evangelists, who were staying at a nearby missionary station. As he described his vision, they were struck by the similarity of its elements to the Revelation of St John, as expressed in the final book of the New Testament. Two passages in particular stood out. The first was:

And the serpent cast out of his mouth water as a flood after the woman, that he might cause her to be carried away of the flood.[*]

This fragment, they thought, was close to Harner's experience of the 'grinning crocodilian head', which had also gushed water. The second passage was even closer:

And there was war in heaven: Michael and his angels fought against the dragon; and the dragon fought and his angels, And prevailed not; neither was their place found any more in heaven. And the great dragon was cast out, that old serpent, called the Devil, and Satan, which deceiveth the whole world: he was cast out into the earth, and his angels were cast out with him.

The missionaries were impressed that a witch-doctor brew could help an atheistic anthropologist experience the same sort of revelation as one of their great saints. But there was, of course, the possibility of a purely psychological explanation. Most people in our Western culture are exposed to Biblical material in childhood, even when their upbringing is not overtly 'religious'. It seemed entirely likely that Harner had absorbed some of the compelling imagery of Revelation and used it to create his own narcotic-induced trance fantasy.

The biologist and author Lyall Watson somewhere

---

[*] King James Version, Revelation 12:15, 12:7–9.

suggests that Harner himself accepted this explanation for a time. If so, he did not hold to it for long. He was still experiencing unpleasant side-effects from the ayahuasca brew and decided to seek out an expert on its effects, an old blind shaman who had used it many times. What happened when he did so was as weird as anything Harner had seen in his visions:

> I went to his hut . . . and described my visions to him segment by segment. At first I told him only the high-lights; thus, when I came to the dragon-like creatures, I skipped their arrival from space and only said, 'There were these giant black animals, something like great bats, longer than the length of this house, who said that they were the true masters of the world.' . . . He stared up towards me with his sightless eyes and said with a grin, 'Oh, they're always saying that. But they are only the masters of Outer Darkness.' He waved his hand casually towards the sky.

Harner was stunned. It was obvious from his conversation that the world he had visited was well known to the blind shaman from personal experience. But this meant it could not be a fantasy Harner had created using elements from Revelation or any other source. It had to be an area of objective reality open to exploration by those who took the drug.

In other words, the spirit world that Harner had visited was an actual place.

Spirit Cats

My first experience of the shamanic spirit world followed a lengthy period of esoteric training – nine years of daily meditations and visualisations, culminating in a ritual initiation. I found myself in an environment that could have doubled as a set for a western movie. There were mountains in the distance and a dusty trail winding through a stretch of semi-desert bordered by rocky outcrops and a few straggling bushes. I didn't see the bear approach until it was almost on top of me, a magnificent towering figure with impressive teeth and claws. The reality tone was sufficient to cause me a frisson of fear.

Was this the creature I was there to meet? Was this to be my spirit guide? Frankly, I had expected a cat, possibly a big cat, or at least a dog. But I asked the question I'd been taught to ask and the bear answered in the affirmative. Communication was peculiar. The bear did not speak as I spoke. Neither did it use telepathy in the sense of a voice in my head. Rather there was the transfer of meaning: I somehow knew what the bear wanted me to know.

Over more than sixty years of occult study and practice, backed up by a master's degree in Western esotericism from Exeter University, I learned many of the fundamentals of shamanism, among them that Harner's discovery of an objective spirit world has been supported since the 1950s by the experiences of other anthropologists. It has even managed to achieve a degree of academic credibility, thanks to the work of Carl Jung, one of the founding fathers of modern psychology. Jung's experience as a psychiatrist led him to postulate the existence of a collective unconscious, which he defined as an objective aspect of the human psyche, noted for pre-existent, semi-autonomous patterns of behaviour he named 'archetypes'.

Among the archetypal images he investigated was the eternal feline. Jung believed each of us had an inner cat, which he associated with the anima, mankind's feminine aspect. Since one of the most important psychological tasks of the individual man is to become conscious of his own anima, Jung felt it was productive for his male patients to work with this inner cat, but warned that it could sometimes lead them into patterns of injurious behaviour, notably sexual, because of its feline nature.

Ever-protective of his scientific reputation, Jung couched his ideas in ultra-obscure terminology. But, despite this precaution, his uncomfortable followers soon began to suspect that what he claimed to have discovered was a whole non-physical realm with its own laws and living inhabitants. Given this insight, it is difficult to see how Jung's collective unconscious differs substantially from the ancient concept of a spirit world. Towards the end of his life, Jung finally admitted he now believed the spirit hypothesis provided a better explanation of the phenomena he had studied than his own early theories of psychic processes common to humanity because we all share the same broad pattern of a physical brain.

Jung developed his own method of reaching the objective psyche, a sort of controlled reverie he called active imagination. Shamans employ a variety of techniques – psychoactive botanicals, like peyote, mescaline and the ayahuasca Dr Harner imbibed, sleep deprivation, trance drumming and ritual ordeals among others. The reality tone of the shamanic experience changes with the method used, but results are similar and often include contact with spirits.

Among them are animal spirits.

A common aspect of shamanic training is the discovery of the shaman's power animal, a spirit creature willing to enter into a personal pact. Although details of the pact vary, it will typically involve assisting the spirit in gaining experience of physical reality. In return, the spirit pledges to aid the shaman in activities such as healing or success in the hunt. Since the powers granted are obviously related to the spirit's inherent abilities, cats large and small are among the most eagerly sought-after spirit allies. This is particularly true of tribal communities, who rely on hunting for all or part of their food supply – what better spirit ally could you have than one of nature's best-equipped hunters? And we must remember that we are not dealing with a physical cat, not even the spirit of a physical cat, but an archetypal representative of all cats of a particular type – in other words, a cat god. Could it be that here, at last, we are approaching an explanation of our close relationship with cats?

I have a suspicion that the answer to that question may be yes, a suspicion that will take us on a return visit to that most cat-friendly of all human cultures – Ancient Egypt. But to understand what might have happened there, we need to acquaint ourselves in a little more detail with the shamanic experience that leads to establishing contact with a power animal. Here, drawn from my personal experience, is a simple but effective technique that will allow you to do that today.*

The method requires some equipment and a little preparation. The equipment is a shamanic drum or a CD of authentic shamanic drumming. (Both items are available on-line from the Foundation for Shamanic Studies.†) You will also need a room where you can lie down undisturbed and a friend to do the drumming or take charge of your CD player.

The preparation involves finding your entrance to the Lower World. For this you need to take a walk outside.

---

* Without drugs, life-threatening ordeals or any other scary stuff.
† https://www.shamanism.org/

Keep an eye open for a hole in the ground. What you're looking for is something like the entrance to a badger's sett or a fox's earth, the mouth of a cave, or a hole between the roots of a tree. It's important that this opening is a real place and not something you've made up. It is also important that it feels right to you. Some shamans talk of the entrance 'calling out' to them.

When you find it, you need to examine your entrance carefully, taking note of any distinguishing features. Sketch the hole and its immediate surroundings. Take a photograph on your phone. Try to commit the area to memory in as much detail as possible.

Now go to the room you have chosen, switch off your phone and make sure you will not be disturbed for the next hour. Find a comfortable place to lie down and have your friend begin the shamanic drumming. Tell him to drum steadily for twenty minutes, then speed up for a further five as a signal that it's time for you to come back.

Close your eyes, relax your body, and visualise the opening as vividly as possible, with yourself standing outside it. If it's too small for you to pass through easily, enlarge it through an act of imagination, or shrink yourself to fit. Then step in. You'll find yourself in a passageway or tunnel, leading downwards. Follow it until you come out at the far end. You've now reached what shamans call the Lower World, no less real for being imaginal. If you stay there long enough, you'll be approached by an animal.

In this spirit world, animals can talk (or at least communicate telepathically) and understand what you say to them. When you undertake this journey, you should ask any animal that approaches you, 'Are you my power animal?' If the creature is willing to enter into a pact with you, it will reply in the affirmative. If not, it will simply walk away.

Once you have discovered your power animal and worked out the details of the pact between you, you are free to leave the Lower World, retracing your steps to return the way you came. Your new spirit ally will often accompany you to the entrance of your tunnel, but will not follow you into the Middle World. You should, however, allow it to experience the Middle World on a regular basis by 'dancing your animal'.

This, in its simplest expression, involves making free-form dance movements that mimic the gait of your power animal and permit it to use your senses as gateways to the physical world. More elaborate forms of the dance involve your disguising yourself as the animal by means of ritual costume, often including animal skins.

Since modern Western culture tends to devalue spirit experiences as 'just imagination' and therefore somehow unreal, it is worth noting that shamanism has developed a useful technique for testing the effectiveness of your power animal contact: the Psychic Power Game.

To play the Power Game, you will need a group of people, split into two equal teams, two chicken bones, one with a black cord attached, eight small crystals or similar tokens to use as counters, and two cloths.

Before the game begins, the teams should decide on a suitable prize for the winner. Traditionally this should take the form of a gift from the losers, such as food or a massage. Both teams must agree that the prize is acceptable. Next, each team must select two of its most sensitive members to function as its seer, plus a back-up. This is followed by the selection of a hider, plus back-up. (The meaning of both terms, seer and hider, will become apparent in a moment.) A referee is also appointed.

The teams privately discuss and decide on their strategy for the game and devise a suitable set of signals for use while it is being played since no talking is allowed after the game starts.

A line is drawn on the floor and the two teams are ranged on either side of it, facing one another. Members may approach the line as closely as they wish, but should any part of their body cross it, their team forfeits a counter to their opponents. At the start of the game, all eight counters are held by the referee.

It doesn't matter which team goes first, since both have an equal number of turns. The action begins when the hider from the first team shuffles the two chicken bones around underneath his cloth, conceals one in each hand, then removes his hands from the cloth and holds them out towards the opposing team. The object of the game is for the seer from the opposing team to determine which hand holds the bone with the black cord. He can take as long to decide as he wishes, but is only allowed a single guess. If he succeeds, his team wins a crystal token from the referee; or, if the referee has run out, from the opposing team. This constitutes a game round. When it is completed, the opposing team takes its turn at hiding the bone. The first team to accumulate all eight tokens wins the game.

But this is only the bare bones of the Power Game, which is characterised by several subtle layers. First of all, each seer is encouraged to work shamanically to the best of his, or her, ability. He might, for example, elect to guess with his eyes closed in order to visualise the location of the bone or he might allow himself to pass into a full-blown trance. His team, meanwhile, will attempt to aid the 'seeing' process in accordance with their previously decided strategy (or spontaneously, as long as there is no spoken communication). They might, for example, decide to hold hands, touch bodies, create a cone of power, visualise a shield or engage in chanting.

The hiding team, meanwhile, is free to take any appropriate action they see fit – shouting, screaming, dancing, making animal noises – to put off the opposing team's seer. Their only limitation is that they must not cross or throw anything over the line.

Since the seer has a 50:50 chance expectation of guessing correctly, the results are amenable to statistical analysis. Provided care is taken to safeguard against cheating and/or sensory clues, any team scoring consistently above (or below) chance expectation may confidently be deemed to be using psychical abilities. Thus the game may be used as a foundation for solidly based scientific psychical research without, as anyone who has played it will readily attest, boredom becoming a factor.

But, whatever its possibilities, psychical research is not the prime purpose of the game. I have so far been coy about its shamanic aspects. The game is first and foremost a test of power-animal contact. When used as such, the seer is required to use his imagination to call up his power animal and visualise it moving across the line to look for the bone. It is well worth trying this approach for yourself after you have successfully completed the basic shamanic journey. Experience shows that when the seer can set aside his own instinctual responses and rely entirely on his power animal, far better results are obtained than with any other method. Experience also shows that the best results occur when the seer's power animal happens to be a manifestation of Cat. That there can be positive results is in itself a discovery with implications. The most obvious of these is that a power animal can somehow emerge from what is essentially a mental realm to influence our physical world.

This, then, is a brief description of the fundamental shamanic journey. I have taken it. You can take – and test – it for yourself. It is my theory that one of those who undertook it was an early pharaoh of Egypt.

Shamanic Egypt

A shaman's power depends on two factors. The first is the inherent talents of his spirit ally. All cats are superbly equipped to be hunters, but small cats, as we have seen, also demonstrate psychical abilities, like telepathy, precognition and spirit vision, which makes them ideal for anyone interested in magical shamanic practice. The second is the shaman's own position, authority and, to a lesser extent, natural ability. A tribal shaman will typically exercise power no further than his village and surrounding countryside, whereas a shaman who also happens to be president of his country may reasonably be expected to exert a far wider influence.

But where are we to position a whole civilisation, like that of Ancient Egypt? How much shamanic power might a pharaoh wield? One imagines it would be far-reaching indeed. Throughout its long history, Ancient Egypt was a theocracy. Its pharaohs were not merely kings but deities. Their word was law. Their rule was absolute. Their prestige was sky high, their wealth unimaginable. When they died, they joined the 'imperishable ones', the circumpolar stars, and became one with the gods. A pharaoh who also happened to be a shaman would be a powerful figure indeed, capable of a profound influence on his own culture and others of the ancient world, an influence that might well reach down the centuries, perhaps even to the present day.

But, interesting though it may be to speculate about such a figure, conventional Egyptology teaches there was no such thing as a shamanic pharaoh, no hint of shamanism in the whole of Egypt's long history. Yet, in this instance, there is some fascinating evidence to suggest conventional Egyptology might be just plain wrong.

The first clue to the practice of shamanism in Egypt appeared in 1881 when the French Egyptologist Gaston Maspero discovered what came to be called the Pyramid Texts. These hieroglyphic inscriptions turned out to be a series of spells, or at least utterances, designed to guide a dead pharaoh through the afterlife on his journey to the heavens. At least, that's what the academics will tell you, their consensus opinion sufficiently petrified to be presented as unquestionable truth. But read carefully through the short quotation below, translated from an engraving on the south wall of the sarcophagus chamber of a pyramid at Saqqara:

Atum, this your son is here ... whom you have preserved alive. He lives! He lives! This Unas lives! He is not dead, this Unas is not dead! He is not gone down, this Unas is not gone down! He has not been judged, this Unas has not been judged!°

Notice anything peculiar? This passage doesn't refer to a dead pharaoh at all, but to a living one. The academics have somehow missed the point, even though the passage is repeated *twenty-two times* in the texts, and in one the pharaoh is told to stand up, stir himself and have a beer.

The sentence about not being judged should lay to rest any lingering suspicion that the academics may be right. In Egyptian religion the dead were escorted by the god Anubis to the Halls of Judgment where their souls were weighed against a feather. This had to happen before they could proceed to their reward or punishment. There was no other way for a dead person to continue his journey. Yet the text clearly states that Unas has not been judged. If he was dead, for him to proceed without the final judgment would deny everything the Egyptians believed about the afterlife. The logical deduction, as the text itself insists, is that what is being described here are not the experiences of a dead king but of a living one.

Even though there is no direct reference to cats in any of the inscriptions, the Pyramid Texts are nonetheless vitally important to our understanding of how the furry little beasts took over Egypt. For if it wasn't a dead king being described, what sort of king was it?

° http://www.pyramidtextsonline.com/translation.html

The answer, I would argue, was a *shamanic* king. You have only to read the Pyramid Texts to realise it was the spirit world the Egyptian pharaohs visited, a non-geographical country that exists within the human mind. And there, I think, they met their spirit allies.

The Pyramid Texts date back to Old Kingdom times, somewhere between 2400 and 2300 BCE, but may well reflect an even more distant oral tradition. So you can be sure the earliest shamanic pharaohs were making otherworld trips right at the beginnings of Egyptian civilisation. These were the men, remember, who were looked upon as gods, whose word on everything was law and who, most importantly, were entirely responsible for laying the foundations of Egyptian culture.

Now let's try to work out what might have happened on a warm summer's evening more than four thousand years ago to shift the balance of power in Egyptian culture for ever. What follows is not, of course, the literal truth but, rather, a parable designed to illustrate what must have happened *in essence* between a pharaoh and the Lower World representative of the feline species . . .

Pharaoh Khufu had taken time off from his break-neck building of the Great Pyramid for an important shamanic initiation. He had decided to undertake his first journey to the Lower World to find a power animal that, he hoped, would help him in preserving the *maat*. We don't know exactly how he planned to make the trip, but we can be reasonably sure that, with minor differences – no photographs or CD players, for example – he would have followed the same basic method, outlined above, that shamans use today. So we may imagine with a high degree of certainty that he eventually emerged from an imaginal passageway into the Lower World.

What you find when you enter the Lower World differs in detail from person to person and, indeed, from trip to trip. But for the sake of this speculation we might suppose Pharaoh found himself in a pleasant pastoral environment, not unlike the fertile floodplain of his native Egypt.

Although Khufu hoped to discover his power animal, he knew better than to look for it. It was – and still is – a rule of shamanic journeywork that you must allow your power animal to choose you, not the other way round. So Pharaoh wandered around like a tourist, admiring the scenery and wishing his power animal would get a move on.

As the evening wore on, animals *did* approach him. There was a crocodile that looked particularly promising and later on a hawk, but when he asked, 'Are you my power animal?' they wandered off without replying. Then, just as he was beginning to get desperate, he felt something brush sensuously against his ankle and looked down to find the cutest little bundle of fur looking up at him with big round eyes.

'Are you my power animal?' demanded the pharaoh, joyfully.

'Yes, I am,' said Cat. 'But only on my own terms.' She extracted a sheet of papyrus from under one armpit. 'Please sign this contract in triplicate.'

The besotted Khufu scarcely glanced at it before reaching for his hieroglyphic quill. There was something about god status, something about not letting cats run into fires, something about eyebrows, something about fish on Fridays. There was a fierce amount of small print, which he didn't have the patience to read. Pharaoh signed with a flourish.

When he returned to his palace in the Middle World, he found a cat curled up asleep on his most comfortable throne.

The shamanic contract with Pharaoh proved so successful (from the cats' point of view) that before long it wasn't just a question of shaving your eyebrows when a cat died but, if you were a priest, of shaving your entire body, face and head, whether a cat had died or not. Furthermore, despite a long tradition debarring priests from wearing garments derived from animals,* the high priest found himself obliged to wear a leopard skin as a mark of his office.

But while shamanic practice may explain the extraordinary popularity cats achieved in Ancient Egypt, it's difficult to see how this could have survived the collapse of Egyptian culture two thousand years ago. Our earlier survey of cats through the ages shows clearly how the

* They mostly wore linen, derived from flax.

relationship between cats and humans changed frequently, manifesting as love of cats in one era and hatred of them in another. Ancient Egypt marked a high point in the relationship, unequalled until the present day, but there is no evidence to suggest shamanic practice is currently the reason for the worldwide popularity of cats. For that, we need to investigate an era that predates ancient Egypt by millennia.

Prehistoric Cats

Humanity's earliest encounters with cats were a far cry from the cosy relationship we have formed with the little housebound felines of today. Cats appeared in the depths of prehistory before true humans emerged on the scene; and most of those cats were huge. The modern cheetah, for example, is a pale shadow of *Acinonyx pardinensis*, a giant version of the breed that ranged throughout Europe and Asia during the Pliocene and Pleistocene epochs. Although probably quite similar in overall appearance to its present-day counterpart, it grew to the size of an African lioness and achieved weights up to 331 pounds (150 kilos). Longer legs and larger heart and lungs probably enabled it to match modern speeds.

But the giant cheetah, which became extinct during the last Ice Age ten thousand years ago, was almost a dwarf when compared with some of the big cats that shared the planet with humanity. Fossil remains in Germany, France, Spain, the Netherlands and Britain provide evidence of a European jaguar weighing in excess of 460 pounds (210 kilos). An early breed of lion grew to the size of a Siberian tiger – the largest of the modern big cats – and weighed some 660 pounds (300 kilos).

Several prehistoric cats actually grew substantially larger than today's Siberian tigers. One of them, the *Homotherium* or scimitar cat, ranged across an astounding variety of habitats in Europe, Asia, Africa and the Americas, achieving weights of 880 pounds (400 kilos). They hunted in packs during daytime, and while their favourite prey was mammoth, their speed must have made them an ever-present danger to humans as well. They too became extinct at the end of the last Ice Age.

The largest cat of all time – at least, the largest so far discovered – was *Panthera atrox* or the American lion. This monster, which ranged from Alaska to Peru, was more than eight feet long, stood almost four feet at the shoulder and weighed (depending on the source you consult) anything from 774 pounds (351 kilos) to 1102 pounds (500 kilos).

What, if any, was humanity's relationship with these – and other – gigantic felines? What we know of the cat's position in ancient Egypt relies on the written word. Prehistory, as we have seen, is the vast sweep of time that pre-dates the invention of writing. But we may still extract important information from a source that is just as reliable in its own way as text, albeit more subject to interpretation. That source is cave art.

On a chilly day more than twenty thousand years ago, in what is now north-eastern Spain, a solitary figure crawled along a narrow corridor in the dark, inaccessible depths of a rambling cavern complex. She[*] was smallish in stature, stockily built and plump, heavily wrapped in animal skins and furs. Her face was pale and flat, with narrow eyes, like those of the modern Inuit. She lit her way in the darkness with a shallow stone saucer-lamp burning animal fat.

There was a medicine bag strung round her neck with a length of sinew-gut cord drawn perhaps from an ibex. In it were sticks of charcoal, and mineral pencils of yellow ochre, red ochre, manganese and iron oxide, along with damp clay, some tuberous roots and several twigs chewed at one end to produce a collection of fibrous brushes. In another pouch, much more heavily wrapped in insulating skins, was water, in the form of a small block of ice.

The woman reached the end of the corridor, now tapered to such narrow confines that it was little larger than a crack in the surrounding rock. She placed her stone lamp on a convenient ledge and began to extract the brushes and pigments from her bag. One imagines she might have hesitated, perhaps even voiced a prayer, but eventually she began to paint. Her picture, outlined in black and red on the cavern wall, was drawn from memory and imagination. It showed a hunting lion.

---

[*] Dean Snow, of Pennsylvania State University, argues convincingly that many painted palm prints at cave art sites appear to be of female hands.

Millennia later, in 1879, Don Marcelino de Sautuola raised his torch to examine that same cat and a veritable gallery of prehistoric art so sophisticated in its execution, so technically advanced in style, that experts of his day were universal in their condemnation of the whole find as a modern fake. Then other, similar, painted caverns were discovered and opinions had to be revised. To date, about 340 caves containing art are known. The great majority of European specimens are in France and Spain, but additional examples have been found in Italy, Portugal, Russia and, most recently, Britain, while discoveries of cave art in places like Australia and Indonesia have pushed back the dating to some forty thousand years ago. The paintings in these caverns exhibit various techniques. Some are done in outline only. Others are filled in with a flat wash, or shaded in colours. Drawings can be seen, made by dipping the fingers in wet clay or paint. The colours used were ground from natural deposits of mineral ore and mixed with animal fat, vegetable juices, water or blood, then applied with a stick or brush.

Animals were the favourite subject matter. Those artists who followed our cave-woman into the Altamira cavern depicted bison, ibex, stags, chamois, aurochs, horses and examples of what appear to be large felines. But many symbols – lines, spirals, zigzag abstractions – and some masked human figures have also been found. While theories abound – magical or religious explanations are by far the academic favourites – no one knows for sure the purpose of cave art.

Today, of course, art is used to decorate our homes and, more formally, as a display designed to elevate the human spirit. This cannot have been the case in prehistory. Painted caverns, like those at Altamira, give no indication of having ever been used as habitations. Even the notion of a primitive art gallery does not bear examination. While sculpted cave art is generally found in shallow rock shelters or near cavern entrances, most paintings are found deep inside. At Niaux in France, for example, the first paintings are about 600 yards (550 metres) from the entrance. From cave mouth to the great fish at La Pileta cave, Spain, is even further — about 1,300 yards (1,190 metres). A major feature of another cavern is so inaccessible that it requires you to

LAST FAREWELL

'In ancient times cats were worshipped as gods; they have not forgotten this'. Terry Pratchett.

risk life and limb swinging out from a natural window with one foot on a tall rock spur before it can be seen at all. Manifestly, these artworks were not meant for general viewing.

Yet they were not casual creations either. An enormous amount of effort went into their composition. The artists often – indeed usually – worked in cramped, difficult conditions. Some paintings are so high that ladders or scaffolding obviously had to be used; no mean feat in a pre-technical culture. The paints were applied in gloom and semi-darkness, by the flickering of torchlight or animal-fat lamps. Smoke smudges can still be seen on the walls.

The artworks themselves were intricate. They might be carved in high or low relief, modelled in clay, or engraved deeply or finely, then hatched. The animals depicted were executed with a skill and grace that suggests a substantial investment of time.

One wonders where the artists found the leisure to produce such masterpieces. They lived in interesting times, the heart of the Pleistocene Ice Age. The whole of Scandinavia lay beneath a single ice sheet, like much of today's Arctic. Almost all of northern Europe was devoid of woodland, chill wastes of tundra broken only rarely in the most sheltered spots by a straggle of pinewood. The Baltic Sea was cut off from the North Sea and existed as little more than a deep, brackish lake. The Gulf Stream was diverted south. The area where London now stands was an open steppe, inhabited by mammoth, bison, woolly rhino, lion and hyena. So much water was locked up in glaciers that sea levels were substantially lowered – the British Isles were joined to continental Europe, Australia linked with New Guinea, Sumatra, Borneo, Java and the Philippines attached to South East Asia, and there was a land bridge across the Bering Strait, allowing the colonisation of the Americas.

For our cave artist, the immediate environment was harsh, similar in many respects to semi-glacial Siberia today. Great herds of bison and reindeer roamed the plains of central and western Europe, as did now-extinct species, like the mammoth and the woolly rhinoceros. Small, nomadic bands of hunter-gatherers, moving with the herds, lived in open-air encampments of tents and huts, often using mammoth bones to build their shelters since wood was near-impossible to find.

Archaeological excavation of their sites show these people lived on venison, fish and eggs. They used bone and flint spears for hunting, bone harpoons for fishing, bone needles to sew together the furs and skins that kept them warm. They were few in number. Tribal communities were small. Nature was unforgiving. If the hunting and the foraging were poor, they starved. If they entered a cavern occupied by a lion or a bear, they died. If they were careless in an attempt to hunt elephant or mammoth, the creature gored them and they died. If they slipped and broke a bone, they died. If they fell ill, they died. If they were too weak to keep pace with the tribal migrations, they died. Even when health and strength, hunting skills and luck were with them all their days, conditions were so extreme that they still died long before they reached what we would now call middle age.

Yet against these pitiless conditions, people found something so important in art that they took time to paint the insides of several hundred caves. To date, there is no generally accepted explanation.

For more than a century, since Marcelino de Sautuola's dramatic find, experts have voiced their guesses. Footprints around the clay bison at the French cave site of Tuc d'Audoubert indicate a tribal gathering, possibly an initiation rite. At the same time, as we have already noted, much cave art is hidden in gloomy, inaccessible depths where it could not have been seen by more than one or two people at a time. Whatever about Tuc d'Audoubert, initiation ceremonies or other tribal gatherings cannot have been a general explanation. In many sites, there would simply not have been enough room.

Religion has also been put forward. There is a strong inference to be drawn, largely from burial sites, that the people of prehistory did practise a religion. Female figurines, such as the rotund little Venus of Willendorf found near Vienna, suggest a belief system associated with the Great Goddess. But while the Neolithic settlement of Çatalhöyük (*c.* 7560 BCE) in Anatolia provides evidence that such a belief experienced long continuity, it is far less certain that She was celebrated in the earlier cave art. The problem is that both cave paintings and engravings were often executed on top of other work, obliterating or at least defacing it. This is hardly the act of someone honouring a religious figure.

Many anthropologists consider that the artworks were an act of magic in themselves, specifically hunting magic. Belief in sympathetic magic is widespread in primitive communities today, so it seems reasonable to assume it was equally widespread in prehistory. The theory of sympathetic magic suggests that if you create a representation of a thing, you can use the representation to influence the thing itself. The notorious voodoo doll of Haiti, the moppet of medieval European witchcraft and the fetish of tribal Africa are all examples of sympathetic magic.

On this basis, the theory is put forward that the paintings were created to influence the success of the hunt. Although few human figures are portrayed, several of the animals are shown transfixed by arrows or spears, which would seem to support the idea. The fact that old artworks were painted over would support it too: fresh magic would have to be made, if not for each hunt, at least for each hunting season.

But there are problems with this theory too. The first, surprisingly, is that the hunt was probably not all that important to Cro-Magnon people. Studies of modern Stone Age cultures, like the !Kung Bushmen of Botswana, indicate that hunting will typically account for only 20 per cent of tribal food. The remaining 80 per cent results from foraging. Contrary to the commonplace picture of hunters tracking game herds every day, !Kung tribesmen hunt strenuously for a week, then put their feet up, metaphorically speaking, for the rest of the month. It is the !Kung tribeswomen who put most of the food on the table.

The second problem is that even if we ignore the relative unimportance of hunting, the art does not entirely work as sympathetic magic. The reindeer is known to have been an important food source, for example, yet it is very seldom pictured. If the paintings were conceived as magical aids to hunting, one would expect reindeer to have been the most prominently featured animal of all.

Then there is the fact that some of the representations are composites. At Pindal, in northern Spain, for example, there is a painting of a trout with the tail of a tuna. Not even the most enthusiastic magician will bother to cast a spell on a creature that does not exist.

Finally, there are depictions of some animals that are simply inedible and so dangerous that it would be folly bordering on lunacy to attempt hunting them for food. Among them are the enormous prehistoric cats.

And therein lies another mystery.

The Cave Art Mystery

There is an extraordinary artwork on the wall of the Chauvet cave in France. Dated back at least twenty thousand years, it depicts a bull on the right-hand side and a cat on the left. To judge from the proportions of the bull, the feline is one of the larger cats, perhaps a lioness. The two animals appear to be copulating, an impression strengthened by the fact that their combination creates the unmistakable image of a human vulva.

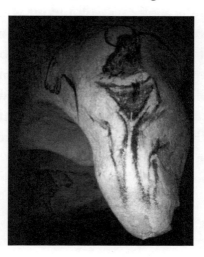

It is difficult to determine the purpose of this picture. As we have seen, a consensus of conventional wisdom has it that the function of cave art is magical. Specifically, it is seen as an act of sympathetic magic, a primitive form of thinking, which speculates that like influences like. Thus depictions of a bison herd might be supposed to attract game. Aurochs pierced by arrows would guarantee the success of a hunt. And so on.

But the graphic in question does not sit neatly with this interpretation. Cats were never eaten by prehistoric man. They were hunters, not prey. And while cattle *were* eaten, by great cats and humans alike, the cat in this picture is not hunting the bull – far from it.

It might seem reasonable to argue that the sympathetic magic involved here was not the sorcery of the hunt, but rather the alchemy of fertility. Yet bulls do not mate with cats – a fact well-known to ancient humanity – and if they did, no offspring could result. Poor sympathetic magic indeed.

Elsewhere in the cavern is another feline representation, the so-called *Panel of Lions*. At the time of its discovery (December 1994) it was the oldest known example of cave art in the world, dated somewhere between 32,000 and 30,000 BCE. It depicts a hunt by a pride of lions. Their prey are horses and rhinos. All the big cats are facing left, a detail shared by the cat-and-bull graphic. Throughout the cave, the predominant animals are also felines.

Not all cave art is representational, of course. Perhaps

the artwork of the bull and the cat is less a mystery than a whimsy, something akin to a doodle by the artist with no more serious purpose than decoration. There was a time when such a theory might have been accepted by archaeologists – and readily – but recent discoveries have shown that prehistoric depictions were a serious, sophisticated business that would never have been undertaken lightly.

Since 1981, the American biochemist Dr Steven J. Waller has promoted the theory that there is an acoustical element to deep cave art. Over the years, he has devoted a great deal of his professional time to investigating rock-art sites throughout the world. Typically, his work involves producing a percussion sound and recording the echo. Comparison of the data has shown that the artworks are not randomly placed but often reflect the acoustic characteristics of their sites. Where the phenomenon occurs in the open, the echo from a painted site is on average eight decibels louder than background level. In deep caves, like those in the famous galleries at Lascaux, the effect is even more pronounced, with readings running between 23 and 31 decibels.

But Waller's discoveries were not confined to the volume of the echoes. It seemed that the acoustic properties of certain surfaces actually determined the type of artwork that would be painted on them. According to a report in the *New Scientist*,* where hoofed animals were

---

* Steven J. Waller, 'The Acoustics of Rock Art', *New Scientist*, 28 November 1992.

depicted it became possible to manipulate the echoes to mimic the sound of a running herd. Even more intriguing, where the graphic depicted a human, the echo of visiting voices appears to emanate from the drawing itself.

This latter phenomenon has led to speculation that our prehistoric ancestors, having heard voice echoes emanating from specific areas of rock, mistook them for spirits and marked the site accordingly. Rituals would then be held, during which early musical instruments, like drums or bird-bone flutes, would appear to evoke the spirits: an example of the primitive mind mistaking a natural phenomenon for magic.

But there is mounting evidence that the prehistoric mind was not as primitive as all that. The assumption made by most palaeoacoustic scientists today is that prehistoric man just happened on places with natural acoustical properties and reacted to them accordingly. Yet there is ample evidence that ancient humanity had a far better grasp of acoustics than that.

Malta's famous prehistoric burial temple, the Hypogeum, is carved from solid rock. Ritual niches cut into the walls of the central chamber are so ingeniously fashioned that if you climb into one it immediately reflects the sound of your heartbeat back at you. The ancient Mayan civilisation of what is now Mexico had acoustical techniques that baffle today's scientists. Clap your hands beside the staircase of the Kukulkan temple pyramid at Chichén Itzá and the call of the sacred quetzal bird will chirp back at you. Stand at its base and shout: a piercing shriek will echo back as a reminder of the human sacrifices once carried out on the summit. Whisper at one end of the nearby ball court and your words will be clearly heard at the other, some 500 feet away. The sound waves generated by your voice are unaffected by wind direction or time of day. Archaeologists involved in the reconstruction of the site noted that the effect improved as their work progressed, but scientists are completely at a loss to explain how such results were achieved.

Traces of a lost 'science of sound' may be found in the depths of prehistory and far from Mexico. Academic Aaron Watson of Reading University discovered a Neolithic stone circle in Scotland ingeniously designed to reflect local sound to its own centre. Today, ultra-sound is widely used in physiotherapy to ease cramped muscles and speed the healing of fractured bones. Was Dr Watson's megalithic circle erected as a healing machine? The suggestion may seem fanciful, but what are we to make of the fact that megalithic chamber after megalithic chamber tested at random throughout England and Ireland displayed a resonance in the 95 to 120 Hertz band, with most in the 110 to 112 range, *despite considerable variation in the sizes and shapes of the chambers*? That the phenomenon goes beyond simple coincidence is confirmed by the fact that in some sites features have been specifically added to bring the chamber into the 110 kHz resonance. Nor is it likely to be coincidence that a 110 kHz resonance stimulates a brain-wave pattern associated with deep relaxation.[*]

The implications of these findings are far-reaching. They point to the existence of a sophisticated prehistoric science of acoustics, lost and unsuspected down the centuries, possibly developed as a healing art. Clearly it was a science of considerable importance to our distant ancestors, for they went to great pains to preserve the knowledge of its practice in such a way that it has remained accessible for tens of thousands of years.

Part of that preserved knowledge is an unexpected association with cats, whose images mark key points in the caverns where they are painted. The study of prehistoric acoustics is very much in its infancy, so we are still a long way from unlocking its secrets, but we might reasonably assume an investigation of acoustics related to cats could bear interesting fruit.

Perhaps it might even unearth our most important clue to the extraordinary relationship between felines and humanity.

[*] See *Time and Mind*, March 2008.

The Symbiotic Cat

Symbiosis is defined as an interaction between two different organisms living in close physical association, typically to the advantage of both. Examples abound in nature. The ocellaris clownfish has made its home among the tentacles of Ritteri sea anemones and fights off attacks by anemone-eating fish. In return, the anemone's stinging tentacles, to which the clownfish is immune, protect it from predators. An even more striking example is the relationship between the shrimp and the goby fish. The shrimp digs a burrow in the sand for both of them, which they move into together. In return for these lodgings, the goby will touch the shrimp (which is nearly blind) with its tail when enemies are about, warning it to retreat into the burrow.

One might be forgiven for suspecting a symbiotic relationship between cats and humanity. They are two very different organisms. They live in close physical association. The advantages to the cat are obvious. The missing element is the advantage to the human. We have searched hard for it, without avail, in the course of this book. But perhaps we have not searched hard enough.

It is a fact of Darwinian evolution that cats – the little ones we now call house cats – have developed a set of personal characteristics that makes them all but irresistibly attractive to humans. Those characteristics, particularly obvious in kittens, are large eyes, short necks and recessive chins. These same features are fundamental to babies of our own species and we are hard-wired to react to them by secreting dopamine – the precise biochemical that floods our bodies when we fall in love. Presented with such a set of characteristics, our instinctive response is to adore, cherish and protect, a natural enough reaction when it comes to our own babies, but to express it towards a wholly alien species, and a predator one at that, suggests we are being manipulated.

This is not, of course, to imply conscious manipulation any more than a flower's bright colouring consciously attracts pollinating insects. What we are discussing is an evolutionary development born of the advantage it brought to cats as a species. It might be argued, of course, that this is where the influence of evolution ends, that the cat's mimicry of human babies is nothing more than a fortuitous coincidence. But how then do you account for what biologists are now calling the 'cuteness factor'?

As we have seen, newborn kittens enter the world blind (eyes tight shut) and almost totally deaf. They are wholly dependent on their mother and recognise their individual feeding teat solely by means of smell. Scientists have discovered that if reared without human contact during this critical period of their lives – which lasts only for weeks – kittens will revert to their ancient feral state and grow up into wild cats. If, however, they catch the scent of a human being during this time, they are programmed by nature to become, all things equal, domesticated cats, fed on the finest fare and occupying the best seats in the house. They do this largely by demonstrating the cuteness factor.

The cuteness factor is a set of behaviours humans find entertaining, amusing or just plain adorable. Although not particularly easy to define, you will find multiple examples on YouTube. See my Electronic 'Bibliography', pages 229–36, ' Cuteness Factor'

Since cats are virtually untrainable, we may safely assume that most of the behaviours depicted in these movies are instinctive (that is, evolutionary developments). Like the cat's physical characteristics, they suggest our reactions are being manipulated.

Pause for a moment to consider what this really means.

Since their first appearance on this planet, cats have followed an evolutionary path designed to create a relationship with humanity in a process so subtle few humans ever even suspect it. They have, in fact, been taking steps towards a possible symbiotic relationship. Should you think I am overstating my case, let me present more evidence.

Ions are atoms or molecules in which the total number of electrons is either more or less than the number of protons, an inequality that generates a positive or negative electrical charge. Both types of ion occur widely in nature; both have a profound influence on humanity. A build-up of positive ions, such as occurs before a thunderstorm, makes us feel dull, tense and listless, often with an accompanying headache. But, by contrast, we tend to feel relaxed, alert and happy when we picnic beside a waterfall, which generates masses of negative ions. We all *love* negative ions.

Stroking a cat produces a cloud of negative ions. The particles are created by the same process of static electricity generated when you rub a balloon with a piece of fur to stick it to a wall.

But would the feelgood factor created by negative ions really justify our suspicions of a symbiotic relationship? The answer, of course, is no. Something much more dramatic would be required. Think of our earlier examples of clownfish and shrimp. Their symbiotic relationships with the anemone and the goby quite literally make all the difference between life and death. Is there any evidence that some similar factor might be present in the relationship between cats and humanity? Astonishingly, the answer here is yes. Furthermore, our prehistoric ancestors might have known about it when they created cave art carefully positioned to link felines with specific sound vibrations and healing: the findings of modern science show beyond doubt that a cat's purr can help mend broken bones.

A leading light in the fundamental research is Dr Clinton T. Rubin, a professor of biomedical engineering at the State University of New York, who for years now has focused his attention on understanding the cellular mechanisms responsible for the growth, healing and homeostasis of bone, cartilage, tendon, ligament and muscle in the human body. His work in this area has led him to publish more than two hundred peer-reviewed papers on, among other things, the use of specific vibrations to promote bony ingrowth into surgical implants and the acceleration of fracture healing. Among his many discoveries is that exposure to frequencies between 20 and 50 Hz leads to an increase in bone density.

Cats purr at frequencies between 25 and 50 Hz with extensions up to 140 Hz. Experimental research has shown that the 25 to 50 Hz range of frequencies promotes bone strength by 20 per cent and not only stimulates the healing of fractures but also the speed at which the healing takes place.

The effect is not confined to bone. Sound vibrations between 50 and 150 Hz administered at low volume have been found to relieve both acute and chronic pain in some 82 per cent of patients.

The laboratory findings are receiving confirmation from medical practice in the field. Vibrational applications within the 20 to 140 Hz range have proven effective in reducing swelling, healing wounds, repairing damaged muscle and tendon, increasing joint mobility and even easing shortness of breath. Russian sports medicine now routinely uses mechanical vibration in the 18 to 35 Hz range to improve the relaxation of strained muscles and increase the stretching ability of tendons.

Thanks to the (largely unreported) work of Dr Rubin and his fellow scientists, the purr of a cat has now been shown to be a general healing mechanism, capable of therapeutic effects across a broad range of conditions. More research is needed into specific uses of particular harmonics and their application, but already there are encouraging results in this area. Cats have, for example, a particularly strong harmonic at 100 Hz – the exact frequency that has been found to decrease the symptoms of dyspnoea, a distressing lung disease.

Nor does it end there. Study after study attests to the extraordinary healing powers of cats without necessarily pinpointing the precise mechanisms by which they bring about their beneficial results. Research continues, but the list of proven benefits is already impressive . . .

A study carried out at Minnesota University concluded that owning a cat reduces your risk of having a stroke by a third.

The same Minnesota University scientists who discovered the part cats can play in reducing the risk of strokes also discovered that cat-owners are less likely to die of cardiovascular disease. The statistics relating to this area are both significant and disturbing. People who live without cats are between 30 and 40 per cent more likely to die from cardiovascular disease than their cat-owning counterparts. Related research suggests cat-ownership significantly reduces the risk of heart attacks.

According to a State University of New York at Buffalo study, cat-ownership also leads to lower blood pressure, while other studies suggest it can boost your immune system, help reduce the risk of developing allergies in young children, and there is even evidence that it may also reduce the risk of developing asthma.

In 2006, a Canadian study not only showed that statistically cat-owners have lower cholesterol than the rest of the population, but also indicated that taking in a cat was actually more effective at lowering cholesterol than conventional medications. Other studies suggest a similar effect on triglycerides: here, too, cat-ownership leads to lower readings.

Although less easy to quantify, many health professionals recognise the profound psychological benefits that flow from having a cat. These include anxiety and stress reduction, mood improvement, and even some help with the ravages of severe conditions like depression.

Cats are now being increasingly used as part of the therapy offered in convalescent homes, with tangible results proven by a subsequent decrease in medical costs. There is even evidence that the introduction of a cat can have a positive influence on the communication problems experienced by autistic children.

Neuroscientist J. Manerling tells the moving story of how his four-year-old autistic son, previously mute, began to have his first-ever conversations with a cat named Clover. Now that the boy is a fully functioning young adult, his father reports:

> Richard has friends, attends college and is not ashamed of having autism. He once told me that he believed all cats have autism because 'Cats are like me. They look at everything and think about it when everyone thinks they are not paying attention and they only talk when they have something to say.'*

A fitting tribute to Clover and the final insight into my theory that evolution has granted house cats and humans a fully functioning symbiotic relationship.

---

* http://cats.about.com/od/youandyourcat/a/catsandautism.htm

Afterword

'You two like cats, don't you?' asked the pump attendant at our local petrol station.

'We do,' Jacks and I admitted suspiciously.

'There's a little kitten been running around here all morning. I think somebody must have dumped him. He won't last here much longer with all the cars coming and going.' She looked at us expectantly.

We muttered excuses about already having far too many cats. Couldn't possibly take on another.

'Would you like to see him?' she asked brightly.

He was the most adorable little mite you've ever seen, so small he could stand on the palm of my hand. And purr. We were on our way to the accountant's at the time, but somehow the car turned itself around and drove itself home with the kitten. He let us know his secret name at once. Thus did we acquire Cutipuss Rex. The pump attendant gave us a page of Green Shield stamps.

Cutie grew into the most handsome of cats, a little neurotic, but then aren't they all? At the fullness of his life, for reasons never altogether clear, his lungs began to fill with fluid. Noreen, our vet, operated to drain them but they began to fill again within days. 'I'm afraid there is no hope,' Noreen said. We left the surgery in tears. Noreen refused to charge for her services.

Wug-wug, The Maggot's wife, had an easier passing. In old age she developed kidney problems, lost weight painlessly until she became a fairy cat and finally died fast asleep in her favourite spot beside the stove while we entertained a guest for a lunch.

The Maggot survived until the age of ten, when he became the happiest cat on the planet following the extraction of a painful tooth. He wandered off to celebrate and never came back. My friend Jason insists he's still out there somewhere, following his maggoty ways. I live in hope and sometimes tears.

Whatever the circumstances, it is always hell to lose a favourite cat, but there may be some solace to be had from the work of René Schwaller de Lubicz, a scholar of ancient theology, mystical thought and esoteric symbolism.

Schwaller taught himself to think like an Egyptian when he spent many years in the detailed study of Egyptian temple architecture, which he firmly believed was based on the proportions of the human frame. Gradually, year by year, he increased his understanding of the Ancient Egyptian mind and, in so doing, unlocked the symbolic secrets that underpinned the Egyptian worldview. Gradually, year by year, he developed an esoteric worldview of his own.

His insights were fascinating. He conceived of a cosmos that emanated from a single powerful mind, as taught in the Hebrew Kabbalah and emphasised in the symbolism of Ancient Egypt and modern shamanism. Great creative principles weave through space and time to coax our world into manifest existence. As human beings, we share this mental ocean with those same principles – often experienced as gods – with one another and with animals. During the process of creation, anatomically modern humans evolved out of animal life by incorporating the evolutionary impulses of other species. Thus, we are part bull, part lion . . . and part cat.

You must be mad or you wouldn't have come here. Tenniel illustration to Alice in Wonderland.

Because of this, contemplating the symbol of, say, an eagle – in, for example, a Pyramid Text – can help us become conscious of the eagle spirit working through us. The symbol activates an innate knowledge of flying and even stimulates our memory of it at earlier stages of our own evolution. In exactly the same way, you can also tune into your inner cat and in the process strengthen your fundamental links with the universe.

So Jason could be right. The Maggot may still be out there, no longer patrolling his night range, but wandering the depths of my symbiotic soul.

I certainly hope so.

Electronic 'Bibliography'

Over a writing career that spans more than half a century, I have become accustomed to carrying out my research in libraries, including my own. Even the advent of the internet failed to change my immersion in books: it merely gave me access to more of them through online libraries.

But as I began preparations for the current opus (pun intended) it occurred to me that I might have been missing something. Surely the internet was not only a road to library information, but also a source of information in itself. Furthermore, the information it contained – in the form of blog entries, sales pitches, opinionated articles and the like – would be of an entirely different flavour to that contained in academic tomes. Perhaps no bad thing, given the subject matter of my book.

I realised, of course, that the internet is nothing if not unreliable, that I would have to use considerable discrimination in what I accepted and what I rejected. But then, when you come to think of it, the same applies to books and, ultimately, an author who produces a new book sourced from old books must take responsibility for his choices.

All this is to explain the quotation marks around *Bibliography* in the headline above. While writing the present work, I did indeed consult a few books. But only the barest handful. All other research was carried out knee-deep in the mighty swamp of information and misinformation that is the Net. As always, I stand by my choices, but it would be grossly unfair to expect you to accept them without access to my sources. Many of the most important are already presented in the form of footnotes throughout the text, but many more influenced my thinking, if sometimes only a little, and so deserve to be cited.

Since without books my citations cannot follow the usual academic conventions, I have elected to supply you with a 'bibliography' of websites consulted, interspersed with what I hope will prove to be a few helpful notes. Not all the information presented in these sites has found its way into my book, but all of it found its way into my head. I can guarantee you will be well entertained and perhaps a little informed if you care to dip into them.

Just don't expect many books in there.

Cats . . .

Ancient history of the cat: http://www.ancient.eu/article/466/
Cat ownership reduces risk of strokes and heart attacks by more than a third: *Telegraph* March 19 2008 (The study looked at 4,435 adults aged between 30 and 75, about half of whom owned a cat.) http://

www.telegraph.co.uk/news/uknews/1582144/Owning-a-cat-cuts-stroke-risk-by-third.html

Cat trip ups: http://edition.cnn.com/2009/HEALTH/03/27/fall.dogs.cats/

Cat worship: http://www.catster.com/lifestyle/6-cat-gods-goddesses-worshiped-ancient-cultures

Cats as guardians of the Egyptian Underworld: https://prezi.com/rvq-vk-6upgn/egyptian-cats-guardians-of-the-underworld/

Cats cause extinctions: https://en.wikipedia.org/wiki/Feral_cat

Dusty had 420 kittens: http://www.guinnessworldrecords.com/world-records/most-prolific-cat

First cat in space: http://history.nasa.gov/animals.html

Hypnotist cat: https://www.youtube.com/watch?v=u_vlbexyGr0

Unsinkable Sam: https://en.wikipedia.org/wiki/Unsinkable_Sam

French village called Pussy: https://en.m.wikipedia.org/wiki/Pussy,_Savoie

The cat in history: http://www.thegreatcat.org/category/cat-in-history/

Devotional cat school within Hinduism. Surrender to God like a carried kitten and let him carry you across the ocean of samsara: http://hinduwebsite.com/hinduism/essays/sacred-animals-of-hindu-ism.asp

Folklore about cats: http://messybeast.com/folktails.htm

Cat Síth, the Celtic myth of a faerie cat: https://en.wikipedia.org/wiki/Cat_sìth

Cats in (largely Persian) mythology and folklore: http://www.iranicaonline.org/articles/cat-in-mythology-and folklore-khot

Charming article on feline folklore which includes the following fable . . . 'According to an old legend, cats were the only creatures on earth who were not made by God at the time of Creation. When God covered the world with water, and Noah set his ark afloat, the ark became infested with rats eating up the stores of food. Noah prayed for a miracle, and a pair of cats sprang to life from the mouths of the lion and lioness. They set to work, and quickly dispatched all the rats — but for the original two. As their reward, when the boat reached dry land the cats walked at the head of the great procession of Noah's animals. Which is why, the legend concludes, all cats are proud, to this very day.': http://www.endicott-studio.com/articleslist/feline-folklore-by-terri-windling.html

Worldwide cat folklore: https://www.cuteness.com/blog/content/cat-folklore-legends-from-around-the-world

The Cait Sidhe, some cat tales from Celtic folklore: http://www.play-fulkitty.net/2014/03/17/cats-in-history-celtic-folklore/

Cats in world mythology: http://pio.tripod.com/magicpaw/catmyths.html

Detailed, interesting article on cats in folklore and religion, originally delivered as a lecture to an Australian branch of the Theosophical Society: http://www.theosophydownunder.org/library/theosophical-lectures/cats-in-folklore-and-religion-by-jennifer-pignataro/

Lucky (or not) black cat: http://americanfolklore.net/folklore/2014/03/why_is_a_black_cat_bad_luck.html

Witchy article on cats in Celtic lore: http://livinglibraryblog.com/?p=977

Evil ghost cats in Japanese mythology: http://www.ancient-origins.net/myths-legends/beware-cat-tales-wicked-japanese-bakeneko-and-nekomata-part-1-004471

Slavic cat mythology: http://www.slavorum.org/cats-in-slavic-mythology-and-folk-tradition/

The cat in folklore: http://www.bartleby.com/234/5.html. Cats in Ancient Egypt: http://kids.nationalgeographic.com/explore/cats-rule-in-ancient-egypt/

Cats' 'superhuman' abilities. Fun piece, but well observed: http://healthypets.mercola.com/sites/healthypets/archive/2015/06/18/13-magical-cat-abilities.aspx

Glow in the dark cats: http://www.bu.edu/synapse/2012/02/29/glow-in-the-dark-cats/

More than 95% cat DNA shared with tigers: http://www.theguardian.com/lifeandstyle/2004/nov/06/weekend.justinehankins

Myths and legends of the Norwegian forest cat: http://eggpen.com/mythology-and-legends-of-the-norwegian-forest-cat/

Secret healing powers of cats: http://www.innerself.com/content/living/home-and-garden/pets-you/4629-cats-and-you-by-caroline-connor.html

Symbolic meaning of cats: http://www.whats-your-sign.com/cat-animal-symbolism.html

Ten amazing abilities of cats. No. 10.reads, 'They help us live longer and healthier. Certainly, both dogs and cats fill our hearts with love

– and help protect it, too. Numerous studies show that no matter their preferred species, pet parents have better rates of blood pressure, cholesterol and triglyceride than those without pets. But before crediting the exercise that comes with daily dog-walking, consider that some research finds that cat owners may have a slight edge over their canine-caring counterparts. One study indicates that cat owners were 40 percent less likely of having a heart attack than those in feline-free homes – better than the heart-protective effect of having a dog.': http://www.philly.com/philly/blogs/phillypets/ 20140416_PET360_10_Amazing_Abilities_of_Cats.html

The power of the purr: http://iheartcats.com/the-healing-power-of-cats /

The science of healing from cats: http://www.the-wayfarer.com/index. php?option=com_content&view=article&id=223%3Athe-science-of -healing-from-cats-part-2&catid=8%3Aarticles&Itemid=8

Wampus Cat legend: http://americanfolklore.net/folklore/2010/08/the_ wampus_cat.html

Cuteness Factor

https://www.youtube.com/watch?v=fNodQpGVVyg&ebc=ANyPxKpB LeGm4OxGb1oE1GwxkckIsyNWXVGwTH6vJYoxrFmPAqPB 9MaLPKq_hiD-3V2HzoFmuxYWFQbCZqvHB4CM2AoZcWredw

https://www.youtube.com/watch?v=q1dpQKntj_w

https://www.youtube.com/watch?v=G8KpPw303PY

Tiger . . .

Goddess of Mercy – page 266/7: http://www.gutenberg.org/files/15250 /15250-h/15250-h.htm:

Interesting article: http://voices.nationalgeographic.com/2014/04/09/ why-have-tigers-been-feared-and-revered-throughout-history/

Japanese tiger attack on Pearl Harbour: http://blog.alientimes.org/ 2010/02/the-tiger-in-japanese-history-and-culture-a-brief-look/

Kids' synopsis: http://www.kidsfortigers.org/index.php?option=com_ content&view=article&id=40&Itemid=79

Myth: http://www.tiger.com.np/myth.htm

Mythology of tiger peoples: https://japanesemythology.wordpress.com /mythology-of-the-tiger-peoples/

National Geographic tiger piece: http://voices.nationalgeographic.com
/tag/talking-tigers/

Nice Hindu myth: http://www.tigersafari.net/tiger-in-indian-myth-
ology.html

Origin of the tiger: http://journal.oraltradition.org/files/articles/16ii/bai
_gengsheng

Poems: http://www.tiger.com.np/poems.htm

Thailand's tiger temple, the target of controversy as I write, with accus-
ations of tiger farming: https://www.youtube.com/watch?v=
VDFhR0nxUnk . . . https://www.youtube.com/watch?v=
P5SUxmi3Qng Calming tiger via 3rd eye:https://www.youtube.com
/watch?v=9X33VE8pL_I

Tiger legends: http://www.earthprotect.com/index.php/media-gallery/
mediaitem/1577-tigers-myths-legends

Tiger lore: http://www.thehindu.com/books/myth-and-lore-of-the-tiger
-down-the-ages/article874729.ece

Tiger worship in Hunan province, China: http://english.cri.cn/7146/
2009/10/21/1881s524016.htm

Tigers in culture: http://www.tigers.org.za/tigers-in-culture-and-folk-
lore.html

Lion . . .

Constellation of Leo myth: http://www.gods-a nd-monsters.com/
constellation-leo-myth.html

Cultural depiction of the lion: https://en.m.wikipedia.org/wiki/Cultural
_depictions_of_lions

Lion myth: http://everything2.com/title/Lions+in+mythology

Lion of Judah: https://en.m.wikipedia.org/wiki/Lion_of_Judah

Lion symbols from prehistory to Narnia: http://tigertribe.net/lion/lion-
in-culture-symbols-and-literature/

Nemean Lion: http://www.greekmythology.com/Myths/Monsters/
Nemean_Lion/nemean_lion.html

Rastafarian mane: https://www.newscientist.com/blogs/shortsharpsci-
ence/2012/10/haile-selassie-lion.html

The Power of Myth, Bill Moyers and Joseph Campbell. Here are some
excerpts from the transcript . . . 'A third position, closer than
Gawain's to that of the Buddha, yet loyal still to the values of life on
this earth, is that of Nietzsche, in *Thus Spake Zarathustra*. In a kind

of parable, Nietzsche describes what he calls the three transformations of the spirit. The first is that of the camel, of childhood and youth. The camel gets down on his knees and says, "Put a load on me." This is the season for obedience, receiving instruction and the information your society requires of you in order to live a responsible life. But when the camel is well loaded, it struggles to its feet and runs out into the desert, where it is transformed into a lion – the heavier the load that had been carried, the stronger the lion will be. Now, the task of the lion is to kill a dragon, and the name of the dragon is "Thou shalt." On every scale of this scaly beast, a "thou shalt" is imprinted: some from four thousand years ago; others from this morning's headlines. Whereas the camel, the child, had to submit to the "thou shalts," the lion, the youth, is to throw them off and come to his own realization.And so, when the dragon is thoroughly dead, with all its "thou shalts" overcome, the lion is transformed into a child moving out of its own nature, like a wheel impelled from its own hub. No more rules to obey. No more rules derived from the historical needs and tasks of the local society, but the pure impulse to living of a life in flower': http://billmoyers.com/content/ep-4-joseph-campbell-and-the-power-of-myth-sacrifice-and-bliss-audio/. . . More Moyers and Campbell: http://www.obooksbooks.com/2015/4051_38.html – In the third episode of The Power of Myth, Bill Moyers and mythologist Joseph Campbell discuss the importance of bears, lions, elephants and gazelles in cages in our zoos: http://billmoyers.com/content/ep-3-joseph-campbell-and-the-power-of-myth-the-first-storytellers-audio/

Yaqui myths and legends – the lion and the cricket : http://www.sacred-texts.com/nam/sw/yml/yml41.htm

Panther, Jaguar, Leopard . . .

Big cat shamanic medicine: http://spiritlodge.yuku.com/topic/868/PantherLeopardJaguar-Medicine#.V2_mwdRemK0

Black panther spirit interpretations: http://www.crystalwind.ca/animal-totems/spirit-of-black-panther

First person experience of shamanic jaguar medicine: http://shaman-portal.org/article_details.php?id=66

Jaguar mythology: http://www.oneworldjourneys.com/jaguar/jag_myth/body.html

Jaguar shamans: http://www.jamiehall.org/jaguar.html

Jaguar symbolism: http://www.pure-spirit.com/more-animal-symbolism/306-jaguar-symbolism

Jaguars in Mesoamerican cultures: https://en.m.wikipedia.org/wiki/Jaguars_in_Mesoamerican_cultures

Panther, leopard and jaguar as totems: http://www.globallightminds.com/2011/11/totems-panther-leopard-jaguar/

The jaguar in Mexico: http://www.mexicolore.co.uk/aztecs/flora-and-fauna/jaguar

Traditional knowledge of the jaguar shamans: http://www.unesco.org/archives/multimedia/?s=films_details&pg=33&id=2186

And finally . . .

How God created dog and cat. This story says it all: http://www.thewayfarer.com/index.php?option=com_content&view=article&id=122:the-origin-of-pets-dogs-and-cats&catid=8:articles&Itemid=8

Appendix: Suitable Names for Cats

Old Possum got it right. Cats really do have two names: the one they are known by and a second, secret, name known only to themselves. But even their known name is a bit of a mystery, as you'll realise if you've ever tried to name a cat. Some monikers just won't stick. No matter how often you call, 'Here, Tiddles,' the cat will ignore you. And the wrong name is worse than no name at all. Any cat will answer to 'Hey, you,' if there is food on the go, but the wrong name, even if it is his known name, is considered way beneath his dignity.

Which is why I have created this special list. Next time you have to name a cat, don't waste your precious time beating your brains to a pulp trying to find something he will accept. Instead, blindfold yourself and stick a pin in the list at random. Whatever it selects will be a perfectly suitable name for a cat, whatever he tries to tell you. If he refuses to accept it, tell him he's on half-rations until he learns sense. That usually does the trick.

Abel
Akhenaten
Alan
August
Baggypants
Barb
Basil
Bimbo Rug
Blackie
Blue
Bob
Bodger
Bonzo Dog Do-dah Cat (may be
    shortened to *Bonzo*)
Broccoli Cat 1
Brutus
Bunny
Caesar
Calico
Campus
Captain Cat
Carrot
Catapult
Catmandu
Cauliflower
Charismatic Banana
Cholmondley
Cindy
Claws
Clogs
Cuddles
Cutipus Rex
Daisy
Diddler
Dog
Doldrums
Doodlums
Dollar
Doodle
Dopey
Driver
Edgar Allen Cat

Felix
Fidelius
Fido
Fiona
Fluzball
Forum
Fred
Gem
Gemini
Geoffrey
George
Gingie Jedge
Grampus
Grizelda
Grumpy
Guzzleguts
Hannibal
Hatfield, Herts and the North.
    Hatters for short
Happy
Hodge
Hopeful
Hornbeam
Howler
Jaws
Jemima
Jenny
Jewel
Juniper
Jupiter
Kitty
Kritten Krong
Lady
Larkin
Leo
Ling
Little Madam
Loot
Lucy
Lugs
Maggot
Manfred

APPENDIX: SUITABLE NAMES FOR CATS

Marmite
Martin
McCafferty
Mermaid
Milton
Miro
Moby Cat
Moonbeam
Mordecai
Mossy-Moss-Moss
Mot
Muncher
Murdoch
Nectanebo
Ned
Neutron the Scientific Cat
Oh-Humps
Pablo
Phobos
Pickle Wockle
Pip
Pixel
Poppet
Poppy
Pudding
Pushkin
Pyewacket
Quin
Rhubarb
Roger
Sam
Sandy
Scoobydon't
Screwball
Seal
Segment
Sergeant Stripes
Sneezy
Splodge
Spook
Spoon
Spot

Spot
Spresso
Squwiff (pronounced *skew-whiff*)
Star
Stella
Stripes
Sunshine
Suzan
Swift
Tasmania
Text
Thing 1
Thing 2
Tiger
Timothy
Toby
Tom-tom
Toxic Moose
Troy
Turtle
Tyrone
Umble
Uncle
Vera
Waldo
Wally
Whiskers
Whittington
Wilberforce
Wilbur
Wobbler
Worthington
Wug-wug
Xanthus the Magnificent
Yang
Yin
Zapata
Zero